My sincere gratitude to my Lord and Savior, Jesus Christ, who called and equipped me for this project. To my wife, Anita, who patiently prayed and encouraged me throughout this project. This project is engraved with my deepest gratitude to her.

My wholehearted appreciation goes to my Pastors, Dr. Jeff LaBorg, Wayne Davis and Keith Weaver. I thank them for their persevering support, prayers and understanding along the way.

To Mike Jones, which gave me unwavering support in this endeavor, I am forever grateful.

Finally, to my mother, Anna Ruth Wisse, thank you for being a constant source in my life, who instilled in me to be all I could be. I love you.

<u>START FRESH</u>
<u>EVANGELISM</u>

Bo Ambrose

Start Fresh Evangelism

A NEW WAY TO SHARE THE GOSPEL

PUBLISHED *by*
PARABLES
Earthly Stories with a Heavenly Meaning

Title: Start Fresh Evangelism
Author: Bo Ambrose
Copyright © Bo Ambrose
March, 2018

Published By Parables
March, 2018

Unless otherwise specified Scripture quotations are taken from the authorized version of the King James Bible.

Unless otherwise specified Scripture quotations are taken from the authorized version of the New King James Bible.

Quotation (p.12)(p.25) By Dr. Jeff LaBorg Fairview Baptist Church, Corryton, TN.

ISBN 978-1-945698-50-7 Printed in the United States of America

Readers should be aware that Internet Web sites offered as citations and/or sources for further information may have been changed or disappeared between the time this was written and when it is read.

START FRESH EVANGELISM

TABLE OF CONTENTS

Dear Reader,

You hold so much more than just another book about soul-winning or another "how-to-course" to mechanically share a few passages from Holy Scripture. "Start Fresh Evangelism" is not simply another book to guilt believers into sharing their faith. In reality it is a road map to help the reader *s.t.a.r.t* fresh with a renewed passion to share the life changing Gospel of Jesus Christ in a day when so few believers actually do and even fewer are equipped to share the most wonderful news ever given to humanity. Our brother Bo Ambrose has poured his life into this work because he has experienced the difference Jesus makes when we share the Gospel. Bo is not presenting a thesis or theoretical work on what might happen if we share Jesus. He is sharing from his own experience of personally winning countless souls to Jesus and witnessing the undeniable difference that Jesus makes in a life when a person comes by faith to the Cross of Calvary. I am excited for you as you start this journey and make this commitment to "go forth and weeping, bearing precious seed, shall doubtless come again with rejoicing, bringing his sheaves with him (Psalm 126:6). Thank you Bro. Bo for challenging all of us to walk in wisdom (Proverbs 11:30) and be obedient to the command and commission of our Lord to go across the street and around the world with the Good News that Jesus saves!

Sola Scriptura,
Pastor Jeff

Fairview Baptist Church

Dear Friend,

There have been very few people that I have met over the course of my forty years of ministry that have the love and passion to share the gospel as Bo. I have known him for over fifteen years, in which time we have ministered together in teaching the Word, hospital visitation, door to door evangelism and trailer park ministry. God has placed within his heart a burning desire for people to experience the good news of Jesus Christ. He not only wants people to experience the gospel, he also desires that they go forward and share it with others. From that desire "Start Fresh" was born. Bo is not only a brother in Christ but I am proud to call him my friend.

Dr. Michael Jones

START FRESH GOSPEL OUTLINE

Gospel Introduction

Talk about something in common
Their work, Their neighborhood, Their House, Their Church Background

Transfer into the Gospel by asking them a question

Q1.   Ever wish you could wipe away the slate clean and start over?

Jeremiah 10:23 – Lord, I know that people's lives are not their own, it is not for them to direct their steps

Q2.   Have you thought about if you died today, would you go to heaven? Why?

Proverbs 14:12- There is a way that seems right to a man, but in the end thereof are the ways of death.

CAN I TELL YOU SOMETHING THAT I JUST HEARD? IT USES THE ACCROSTIC OF ONE WORD "START"

GOSPEL OUTLINE

"S" – Stop Making Excuses For Your Sin

Proverbs 28:13 – He that covers his sins will not prosper, but whoever confesses and forsakes them will have mercy

"T"- Take A Look At My Past – Did It Honor God?
When you bring peace to your past. You can move forward to the future.   1 Corinthians 6:20- For you were bought with a price: Therefore glorify God in Your Body

"A" – Actions Speak Louder Than Words
Colossians 3:17- Whatever you do in word or deed, do all in the name of the Lord Jesus, giving thanks through Him to God the Father.

"R" – If Life Gets Blurry – Refocus Your Life
Matthew 6:33- But seek ye first the kingdom of God, and his righteousness; and all these things shall be added unto you

"T" – Who Are You Going To Trust? Acts 3:19 – Repent, then, and turn to God, so that your sins may be wiped out

START FRESH LETTER

Dear Friend in Christ,

Welcome to Start Fresh Evangelism. This training is a beginning, a basic guideline, and the tool that can help every believer win souls.

One problem about soul winning is that soul winning, if it is implemented at all in a church, is left up to the few. The great commission – **Matthew 28:18-20** – Then Jesus came to them and said, "All authority in heaven and on earth has been given to me. Therefore go and make disciples of all nations, baptizing them in the name of the Father and of the Son and of the Holy Spirit, and teaching them to obey everything I have commanded you. And surely I am with you always, to the very end of the age"

It is not the great suggestion. Soul winning is something that is, and should be, the quest of every believer.

This is why Jesus came: to seek and save that which is lost. It's time for the laborers to get back to the basics of the Gospel and start winning the lost.

This outline has been tried in the church house, the jail house and door to door evangelism. I truly believe that this training being available in the world today for church leaders who want to equip their people in evangelism, relationships and discipleship all for a closer relationship with God.

This Start Fresh Training has been designed with training material, evangelism outline, line card and with your own design of door to door training. With the proper training and a heart for Jesus it will help you in witnessing as a way of life.

There are people praying for you as you begin this training and to witness as a way of life. Thank you for a passion for lost people and I challenge you to give your time, your heart and a love for Jesus.

Thank you!

Bo Ambrose

Bo Ambrose
Start Fresh Evangelism

START FRESH STATEMENT OF FAITH

The Start Fresh Evangelism Statement of Faith is a broad declaration that with God's Word and the material of Start Fresh Evangelism are considered very important for the furthering of Start Fresh Evangelism.

This evangelism is a means for denominations to unite together in the simple truths and to proclaim the word of God. Start Fresh Evangelism believes:

The Bible is the infallible, inerrant, inspired Word of God.
We believe in the Triune God, (Father, Son and Holy Spirit)
Eternal Life is a free gift received by faith – trusting in Jesus Christ alone for salvation.

We believe that every true believer is commanded by Christ to "Preach the Gospel to every creature and to make disciples of all nations"
Being regenerated by the Holy Spirit is essential for salvation, the lost and the sinful man.

Our Lord Jesus Christ was born of a virgin, lived a sinless life, performed miracles, was condemned by Pilate, Crucified on the Cross, Put in an empty tomb, his body was resurrected from the dead, ascended into heaven and will return again.

We need groups all over the nation and the world to share what we know about Jesus and leading people into a personal relationship with God.

Start Fresh Evangelisms' main purpose is to be obedient to the cause of Christ and to be vitally involved in His commission.

SESSION #1

START FRESH
INTRODUCTION

SESSION #1

INTRODUCTION TO START FRESH EVANGELISM

According to **Acts 1:8- But ye shall receive power, after that the Holy Ghost is come upon you: and ye shall be witnesses unto me both in Jerusalem, and in all Judaea, and in Samaria, and unto the uttermost part of the earth.**

See the **power** to be witnesses is to preach boldly and proclaim the Good News understanding that the Gospel is the power of God unto salvation. We are **carriers** and we are announcers of this Good News Gospel realizing that the goodness of God leads us to repentance.

Our job is not to convict. Our job is to proclaim. The Word of God convicts. **If we attempt to do the work of the Holy Spirit, we will condemn.** The love of God flowing from the lips of a Spirit-filled believer will allow the Word of God to do what it does.

Jesus said in **John 12:32 - "And I, if I be lifted up from the earth, will draw all men unto me."**

John 6:44- No man can come to me, except the Father which hath sent me draw him: and I will raise him up at the last day.

He stands with arms wide open. He says in **Matthew 11:28-30 - "Come unto me, all ye that labor and are heavy laden, and I will give you rest. Take my yoke upon you, and learn of me; for I am meek and lowly in heart: and ye shall find rest unto your souls. For my yoke is easy, and my burden is light."**

The Gospel is **Good** News and must be carried by people who are full of Jesus and the joy of their salvation. People can see if you are real or fake. They can see if you know Jesus personally or have just heard about Him.

Start Fresh is a tool that will help people win the lost at any cost from the crack house to the church house. We are going to shout it from the roof tops until the whole world knows how awesome and how wonderful He is.

If **Eternity** is in our hearts, every second is **valuable**; every chance must be taken to bring in this harvest. Our family, our kids, our spouses, neighbors, our team mates at work. Will you help? We need laborers. Jesus said, "Say not ye, There are yet four months, and then cometh harvest?

Behold, I say unto you, Lift up your eyes, and look on the fields; for they are white already to harvest."

The world will be shaken by the power of God if we have a heart to share. Nations will be awakened and we will see the greatest harvest of souls for the Kingdom of God.

We will use every method and every means to save souls from an eternity in Hell. Hear the cry of the lost as they wander around in darkness. You are the one who will throw out the lifeline. You are the one carrying the light. Your light is shining so that those who are in darkness can find their way.

JOHN 15:16 - "Ye have not chosen me, but I have chosen you, and ordained you, that ye should go and bring forth fruit, and that your fruit should remain: that whatsoever ye shall ask of the Father in my name, he may give it you"

Our Lord shared the gospel with many different people. He understood Nicodemus and the woman at the well, and He used that knowledge in drawing them to Himself (John chapters 3 and 4). Our approach, too, should be personally tailored. As we speak with an unbeliever, we should try to discover what is keeping him/her from salvation. Generally speaking, there are three factors that keep people from belief: **inconsistency about God, fear of God, and hatred toward God,** which includes despising His teachings and His Son.

A witness is one who "*says what he knows and knows what he says.*" Where did Jesus say we were to be witnesses? **Acts 1:8** But you will receive power when the Holy Spirit has come upon you, and you will be my witnesses in Jerusalem, and in all Judea and Samaria, and to the farthest parts of the earth."

Where is your Jerusalem, Judea, Samaria or entire world?

Matthew 28:19-20 records words of Jesus just before He ascended into heaven. What was His commandment to His disciples? **28:19** Therefore **go** and make disciples of all nations, baptizing them in the name of the Father and the Son and the Holy Spirit, 20 teaching them to obey everything I have commanded you. And remember, I am with you always, to the end of the age."

It is important that each of us actively trust the Holy Spirit to direct us in our way and prepare the hearts of men as we seek to share Christ. It is also important that we pray specifically for individuals with whom we share our Savior. As we earnestly seek His leadership and pray for people without Christ, we will develop a "love for souls." This is also an active condition that must be present if we are to be effective witnesses.

SESSION #1A

WHAT DOES THE BIBLE SAY ON WITNESSING AS A WAY OF LIFE?

Out of everything we do, the eternal destination of a person is most important. God's heart is to see everyone spend eternity with Him instead of separated from Him. No matter whether a person chooses your church as their church home, we must do our part to give people an opportunity to be saved by sharing the Good News of salvation.

John 20:21
"Then said Jesus to them again, Peace be unto you: as my Father hath sent me, even so send I you."

To Do What? _Take the gospel_

Mark 16:15-20
"And he said unto them, Go ye into all the world, and preach the gospel to every creature. They shall take up serpents; and if they drink any deadly thing, it shall not hurt them; they shall lay hands on the sick, and they shall recover. So then after the Lord had spoken unto them, he was received up into heaven, and sat on the right hand of God. And they went forth, and preached everywhere, the Lord working with them, and confirming the word with signs following. Amen."

Where did they Preach?
Everywhere

How did they know Jesus was with them?
They trusted Him

Matthew 10:7-8
"And as ye go, preach, saying, The kingdom of heaven is at hand. Heal the sick, cleanse the lepers, raise the dead, cast out devils; freely ye have received, freely give." Who is he talking to? _us_

Who does he want to go?
us – every believer

Proverbs 11:30
"The fruit of the righteous is a tree of life; and he that winneth souls is wise."

Matthew 28:18-19
"Go ye therefore, and teach all nations, baptizing them in the name of the Father, and of the Son, and of the Holy Ghost: Teaching them to observe all things whatsoever I have commanded you: and, lo, I am with you always, even unto the end of the world. Amen."

Why do we need to go?

Jesus Command

Romans 10:14-15
"How then shall they call on him in whom they have not believed? And how shall they believe in him of whom they have not heard? And how shall they hear without a preacher? And how shall they preach, except they be sent? As it is written, How beautiful are the feet of them that preach the gospel of peace, and bring glad tidings of good things!"

II Timothy 1:7
"For God hath not given us the spirit of fear; but of power, and of love, and of a sound mind."

Why are people afraid of sharing the Gospel?

Rejection, inadequate, might make a mistake, push
Someone farther away

Acts 1:8
"But ye shall receive power, after that the Holy Ghost is come upon you: and ye shall be witnesses unto me both in Jerusalem, and in all Judaea, and in Samaria, and unto the uttermost part of the earth."

Who receives this power?
every believer

And when?
at time of Salvation

So GO and share the Gospel to our neighbors, fellow employees, church members, our family, waiters and waitresses. Every where you go, you have a way to share. So Be Bold For Jesus!

START FRESH
Evangelism
JUST DO IT

Every Person has a story.
Every story has an ending.
Every ending is a new
beginning!

SESSION #1B

WHY SHOULD I TELL SOMEONE ABOUT JESUS?

Ask the Lord to break your heart for the lost.

Prayer: Lord, let me see people the way that You see people. Give me a revelation that You have come to seek and to save that which was lost, and that You leave the ninety-nine sheep to go after the one lost sheep. The Great Commission is not the Great Suggestion. I thank you Lord that I have the love of God and the power of God in my life and that I will be an effective witness...in Jesus' name. Amen

Soul Winning is a PASSION, not a Program.

Soul Winning is a LIFESTYLE, not an Event.

Soul Winning is a byproduct of a Revival and the Souls will be the currency of ETERNITY.

Romans 1:16, "For I am not ashamed of the gospel of Christ: for it is the power of God unto salvation to every one that believeth; to the Jew first, and also to the Greek."

Acts 2:21, "And it shall come to pass, that whosoever shall call on the name of the Lord shall be saved

Does this mean that only good people can call upon the Lord?

_____ *NO*

Thank you for making a commitment to be present at this training. It reflects your desire to be obedient to the cause of Christ and to be vitally involved in His commission.

Acts 4:12.

What does this passage say about salvation? _____

The message of this text is clear. It is only through **Jesus**, there is no other way to salvation.

So, if we have been given a commission, and if there is no other way to be saved other than through Jesus Christ, how should these two verses affect the way we live our Christian lives?

The answer is obvious: We should be **obedient** to the commission of Christ and to seek to share with others the good news that salvation is available through Him.

THE WHO, WHAT, WHEN, WHY & HOW OF SHARING

THE WHO

Have you ever asked yourself, "Why should I witness?" Several reasons should come to mind.

- Because Jesus commands you to: "*Go therefore and make disciples of all the nations, baptizing them in the name of the Father and the Son and the Holy Spirit,*" (**Matt. 28:19**). Also, **Ezek. 3:11** says, "*and go to the exiles, to the sons of your people, and speak to them and tell them, whether they listen or not...*" If we have the Holy Spirit in us, then we should be excited about sharing with all we come in contact with.

THE WHY

- You must witness because you love the unsaved (if you don't, you should). The most loving thing you can do is present the gospel in hopes of bringing others to salvation. **Galatians 5:22** lists love as one of the fruit of the Spirits. It is love's nature to give. Take for example **John 3:16**, "*For God so loved the world that He gave His only begotten Son...*" Love gives, and if you have only a small portion of His love, you will want to give to others.

THE WHAT

- Witness because it is a wise thing to do. **Proverbs 11:30** says, "The fruit of the righteous *is a* tree of life, And he who wins souls *is* wise." Now, I know I am not a very wise person. But, since God says I'll be wise to win souls, or try to, then great, let me at it. I want to be wise in God's sight not mans.

THE WHEN

- Witness to keep people from going to hell. Hell is a terrifying place of utter anguish and eternal separation from God. Those who are not saved go there. Witnessing is an attempt to keep them out of hell.

- Witness because it pleases God. Witness so they may find love and fellowship with God **1 John 1:3** – That which we have seen and heard we declare to you, that you also may have fellowship with us; and truly our fellowship is with the Father and with His Son Jesus Christ.

THE HOW

- It frees the sinner from sin, it delivers the lost from hell, and it reveals the true and living God to those who don't know Him.

- Shouldn't we as Christians rejoice too? Shouldn't we weep over the lost? Shouldn't we ask the Lord of the field to send laborers into His harvest **Luke 10:2** - Then He said to them, "The Harvest truly is great, but the laborers are few; therefore pray the Lord of the harvest to send out laborers into His harvest.

- Certainly! The salvation of others is the goal of your efforts. The love of God is your motive.

SESSION #1 C

WITNESSING AS A WAY OF LIFE COMMITMENT

To the best of my ability, and with the Lord's help, I will share Christ as opportunities arise.

I am making a commitment to Start Fresh Evangelism because I desire to be obedient to the Great Commission.

I will be obedient each week to complete the homework assignments

I will attend for the next six weeks the weekly training sessions.

If this expresses your desire, sign your name on the line as a confirmation of your commitment.

To evangelize means to proclaim the good news of the gospel of Christ. Jesus in giving the Great Commission to the eleven apostles says in Matthew 28:19-20, "Go therefore and make disciples of all the nations, baptizing them in the name of the Father, and of the Son and of the Holy Spirit, teaching them to observe all things I have commanded you."

Imagine that Jesus saying these words to eleven of us today and we were one of the eleven. What would be our REACTION? Impossible? Incredible? Absurd? Or Lord don't you see there are only eleven of us? Or would we think "Yes Jesus really means me also." We are also under this obligation to teach others. Jesus had just commanded the eleven to go teach and to teach those who were converted to observe all things he had command them which included that we are also to be taught to go and teach.

Is this your commitment?

NAME: _Glare Gates_____   DATE:_____

SESSION #1 D

HOW DOES THE SPIRIT WORK

"We do not need to fear going anywhere to share the gospel. The success we seek is not our own. It is not determined by our worth or abilities. We seek Christ's success, and that success is determined by His will and authority."

"The spirit of evangelism which is basic in soul-winning cannot endure apart from the presence and power of the Holy Spirit. The Holy Spirit empowers, leads, preserves, and guides the soul-winner. The Holy Spirit makes Christ real to the Christian."

To help the believer understand and apply the work of the Holy Spirit in evangelism

John 14:16-18.

What did Jesus say about the Holy Spirit in **John 14:16-18**?

Answer: • He is the Counselor • He will be with us **forever** • He is the Spirit of Truth • He **lives** in us

Effective witnessing depends upon the work of the Holy Spirit. Without the Holy Spirit, who is the Spirit of Truth, effective witnessing is impossible. By understanding His work, we will be better prepared to share our faith with others.

Let's look at three areas in which the Spirit works.

1. How the Holy Spirit works in a believer's life: In **1 Corinthians 12:13**, Paul tells us that He baptizes us into one **body**. This simply means that each believer has received the indwelling of the Holy Spirit and because of this, we are **all** united into one body: the body of Christ.

In **Ephesians 4:30**, Paul says that the Holy Spirit **seals** us for eternity. This simply means that each believer is eternally secure in Him.

In **Ephesians 5:18**, Paul says that the Holy Spirit **fills** us. This simply means that each believer should consistently walk in fellowship with Jesus and live a life of submission under God's control.

What it means to be filled with the Holy Spirit

Lead the class members now in a time of prayer asking the Holy Spirit to reveal unconfessed sin in their lives, to ask for forgiveness for those sins, and to fill them with the Spirit.

Prayer

How does the Holy Spirit work in an unbeliever's life:

Convicts of Sin

_____

John 16:8-11.

In this passage, what does the Spirit do?

_____

Answer: He convicts of sin, righteousness, and judgment.

In **John 15:26**,

Whom does the Spirit testify?

_____

Answer: He testifies about Jesus.

In **John 3:5-6**,

Who may enter the kingdom of God?

_____

Answer: Only those born of the Spirit.

"We have the best in materials, media, and methods, but we lack spiritual power....We cannot evangelize without God's **power**."

He **gives** the witness boldness (**Acts 1:8**) This empowerment gives us confidence in Christ and enables us to be a bold, loving witness.

He **guides** the conversation, if allowed. **John 14:26**- But the Helper, the Holy Spirit, whom the Father will send in My name, He will teach you all things, and bring to your remembrance all things that I said to you. Do not let the fact that you may not have all the answers prevent you from sharing. **Depend** upon the Holy Spirit and He will give you wisdom and words.

Knowing these truths about the Holy Spirit will help you share Jesus in your relationships with power and boldness.

Jesus went to where the lost people were. He walked in their dust and spoke their language. He lived in their culture and understood their deepest need.

WALK IN THE SPIRIT!!!

IF WE LIVE BY THE SPIRIT, LET US ALSO WALK BY THE SPIRIT!

SESSION #2
MY TESTIMONY

AND THEY OVERCAME HIM BY THE BLOOD OF
THE LAMB AND BY THE WORD OF THEIR
TESTIMONY   REV.12:11

WE CAN'T HAVE A TESTIMONY WITHOUT A TEST

SESSION #2

TESTIMONY

Read 1 Corinthians 9:19-23.

In this passage, Paul is giving us his life's mission statement. He wants people saved and reveals what he considers to be his role in helping them come to Christ.

What do think Paul meant when he said "I have become all things?" Write your answer in the space provided.

Became like them — Built a relationship to win them

What you "become" to someone describes your relationship with that person. As Paul lived out his faith every day, **the lost could easily see that he was different.** Since Paul was ministering through relationships, the lost felt free to ask him why he lived the way he did. They were also receptive to hearing Paul's testimony.

Relationships are like bridges that enable us to cross over in order to share the good news of Christ.

Like Paul, because of these relationships and a God-honoring lifestyle, we may be granted passage into the lives of lost people to discuss spiritual matters.

Read 1 Thessalonians 1:5.

8 Descriptions of a "Becomer"

1. He or she is genuinely concerned for others
2. He or she has died to his or herself
3. He or she keeps his or her eyes on the harvest
4. He or she is willing to go the second mile
5. He or she wants his or her life to bring glory and souls to God
6. He or she knows it is the Holy Spirit's job to convict the sinner of sin
7. He or she knows his or her possessions are to be used for service
8. He or she knows that being a friend is an important part of evangelism

Do You Have A "Most Wanted for Christ "list?

Who do you know in your circle of relationships that is lost?

Your family, Your coworkers ___*Lily*___ ___*Beth*___

___*Rick*___ _____ _____

Your friends, Your neighbors _____ _____

_____ _____ _____

Your acquaintances, Other _____ _____

_____ _____ _____

How do we begin to reach them for Christ?

1. Begin praying for them
2. Build or expand your relationship with them
3. Look for opportunities to talk about spiritual matters

"If you and I believe that Jesus Christ saved us, then why do we keep Him so quiet? _____

What will you "become" to those whose names you have written down to enhance their openness to the gospel? _____

_____

A Witnessing Strategy:

In any conversation, it is very important to be natural. Just be yourself and allow your own unique personality to come out in the conversation. Smile and enjoy people with whom you will have an opportunity to share. Remember, you are reflecting the life and love of Jesus Christ!

Question: When you are in a conversation with someone, what areas are typically discussed?

___*Family, work, activities*___

To witness is really no different than starting any other conversation! You are seeking to build a relationship!

To assist you in this conversation. Use the simple acrostic **C.A.S.T**.to help keep you on track.

Remember: Our goal at this time is to build a relationship.

C - Connect - Seek to make a connection with the person. Talk about the person's background: Where are you from originally? How long have you lived here? Other questions: If you are already acquainted, ask about family members or mutual friends.

A- Actions- Find out about the person's work, hobbies, or interests. You may ask: What kind of work do you do? What do you enjoy doing in your spare time? For students, What courses are you taking? If you notice evidence of their interests such as sports, books, art, and so on, you may ask a question or comment about these. Seek to discover commonalities.

S- Spiritual Matters - This is the real heart of the conversation. Find out whether the person is open to discussing spiritual matters. Here are some Questions you might ask: Would you consider yourself to be a spiritual person? Do you ever think about spiritual things? Some like to use diagnostic questions.

T- Tell Your Testimony- If the person is open to you sharing your testimony, then continue sharing the gospel.

This can be done during the introduction time of the visitation. As you take a little time to begin cultivating a relationship or the right to ask the salvation questions to begin the Gospel.

WRITE YOUR STORY

DO YOU HAVE A STORY TO TELL?

MY TESTIMONY IS PERSONALLY EXPERIENCED, EYE WITNESSED AND FIRST HAND

SESSON #2 A

WRITING YOUR TESTIMONY

WRITING YOUR TESTIMONY

"A personal testimony is difficult to disprove. The experience has happened to you. You are the expert on your own story. The Pharisees had no defense for the simple, testimony of the blind man who had been healed.

Telling your testimony will help the believer understand the importance of what other people can go through to develop and share it with an unbeliever

A personal testimony is one of the most basic tools that can be used for witnessing. It is simply your story of salvation. A personal story/testimony is a personal account of your life before you made a commitment to follow Jesus, how you came to know Jesus personally, and how Jesus has changed your life since you came to know Him personally.

A personal story/testimony is divided into three areas:

1. **My life before my commitment to follow Jesus**. This includes what your life was like before coming to Jesus. Loneliness, lack of purpose, afraid to die and no hope may all be part of your story. It culminates in the discovery that each of us are in need of a change and a recognition that humankind's most basic problem is sin.

2. **How I came to know Jesus personally**. How did this occur in your life? Was it in a worship service that you came to know Christ? How did you discover that God loves you and that Jesus died for your sins? When and where were you when you received Jesus as your Savior? This part of your story communicates the circumstances and events surrounding your life-changing encounter with Christ.

3. **How Jesus has changed my life since I came to know Him personally.** The last part of your story communicates briefly how your life is now different as a result of salvation. Indicate the impact He has had on

your life. You may want to examine statements that you made under point 1 as you write out this portion of your story/testimony.

An excellent model of a personal testimony and its use is found in **Acts 22:3-16**. **Acts 22:3-5** Describes Paul's life before Christ. **Acts 22:6-13** Describes how Paul came to know Christ. **Acts 22:14-16** describes how Paul's life was changed

Characteristics of a Personal Story/Testimony

Your personal testimony is very important: It has authority No one can contest it; it happened to you! It communicates. It is a wonderful resource to communicate the reality of how Christ has changed your life! It relates Everyone alive has a spiritual void that can only be filled by a personal encounter with Jesus Christ. It is powerful God can use your story/testimony to impact lives and to reveal the life and love of Jesus Christ to a lost and dying world.

What if you accepted Christ at a very young age?

1. Focus upon a defining moment in your life when your faith was tested and affirmed

2. Focus upon how Christ has protected you

3. Focus upon the direction your life could have gone

4. Focus upon what Christ saved you from

"God custom designed you with your unique combination of personality, attitude, temperament, talents, and background, and He wants to harness and use these in His mission to reach this messed-up world."

Leader, take a moment and share with the class your own personal story/testimony.

Be brief. Your story/testimony should be no longer than three to five minutes.

Be specific, but leave out unnecessary details.

Try to avoid Christian words that the hearer may not understand.

Make sure that you stress that even though Christ has changed your life, you are still not perfect.

My Story/Testimony Worksheet

1. My life before I made a commitment to follow Jesus:

2. How I came to know Jesus personally:

3. How Jesus has changed my life since I came to know Him personally:

As you practice using your testimony, put your personality into it and feel free to include further transitional statements. Each person with whom you will be sharing will be different. Learn how to smoothly transition from one area to the next.

For example: When you come to a Scripture reference, say something like: "The Bible says," or "I discovered the Bible teaches that" or "God says."

As the Holy Spirit leads, begin to share the first part of your testimony: "My Life Before Making a Commitment to Follow Jesus."

The first part of your story/testimony should culminate in the recognition that you needed a change in your life because of sin.

Every believer could write a book describing the impact that Christ has made in his or her life. However, the attention span of most people is very short. In an effort to keep your presentation brief and to the point, share in a sentence or two the impact He has made.

Examples: • And since then He has become a friend that is always there. • And since then He has brought me peace. • And since then He has brought purpose and meaning to my life. • And since then He has been a daily source of strength.

BEFORE CHRIST	**AFTER ACCEPTING**
FEAR OF DEATH	ASSURANCE OF ETERNAL LIFE
REJECTION	ACCEPTANCE
EMPTINESS	FULFILLMENT
REBELLION	FREEDOM
LONELINESS	FRIENDSHIP
INSECURITY	SECURITY
STRIFE	PEACE
GUILT	FORGIVENESS

The Lord doesn't want anyone to be **lost**. We read in **2 Peter 3:9**, "The Lord...is longsuffering toward us, not willing that any should perish but that all should come to repentance." They can only come to repentance when they know what to do.

We also read in **1 Timothy 2:4**, "Who will have all men to be saved, and to come to a knowledge of the truth." Because of what the Lord has **done** for us, we have the obligation to teach others so they can come to a knowledge of the truth and be saved.

Paul says in **1 Corinthians 9:16**, "Woe is to me if I preach not the gospel." How are we going to answer the Lord if we haven't bothered to tell the good news to others

Our Lord in teaching His disciples, tells them in **John 4:35**, "Do you say there are still four months then comes the harvest? Behold I say to you, lift up your eyes and look on the fields for they are white already to harvest." Our Lord was **speaking** of the spiritual harvest of souls who would be lost in eternity if they are not harvested.

There is an **urgency** to teach the lost for Jesus says in **Matthew 9:37-38**, **"The harvest truly is plentiful, but the laborers are few. Therefore pray the Lord of the harvest to send out laborers into His harvest."** We must work in the Lord's harvest because if we don't then those we could have taught will be lost and we don't want that to happen.

In the first century the good news of the gospel caused such great excitement that **"And daily in the temple and from house to house they ceased not to teach and preach Jesus"** (**Acts 5:42**).

We need to be as excited today. And even when they were being heavily persecuted, some even to death, we read in **Acts 8:4, "Therefore those who were scattered abroad went everywhere preaching the word."**

Question: What could stop us today? _____
We are not being persecuted. We have many more advantages. We have the automobiles, airplanes, cell phones, the Internet, and the printed page.

Question: **Are we without excuse?** _____

Teaching the lost is the work the Lord has commanded each of us to do. Successful evangelism is accomplished one person at a time. Evangelism is not only to be done in distant lands, but we must also teach those near us, our next door neighbors, family or at work. God will be with us as we teach His word to the lost.

We read in **Philippians 4:13, "I can do all things through Christ who strengthens me."** When we do what the Lord says to do we will not fail. WHY??? _He is able_____

When we teach the lost we cause all of Heaven to rejoice. Jesus tells us that there is rejoicing in the presence of the angels of God when one sinner repents **Luke 15:7-** I say unto you, that likewise joy shall be in heaven over one sinner that **repententh**, more than over ninety and nine just persons, which need no repentance.

Luke 15:10- Likewise, I say unto you, there is **joy** in the presence of the angels of God over one sinner that repenteth.

Question: How can we share my testimony if I don't have one?
___We can_____

Question: If making disciples is our mission **Matthew 28:18-20,** how can followers of Christ overcome obstacles to be conduits of grace to the lost?

_____

Some Do's and Don't's on the Testimony

DO'S

- Express the positive benefits of having eternal life
- Use specific examples from your life
- Express the assurance that you have eternal life
- Express your experience of God's Faithfulness
- Identify with your prospects
- Avoid Christian Clichés

DON'T'S

- Don't be preachy in your Testimony
- Don't deal with external material life
- Don't chase rabbits in the testimony
- Don't give the answer on heaven

TIME TO WRITE YOUR STORY. WRITE YOUR TESTIMONY AND GIVE TO YOUR INSTRUCTOR BEFORE YOUR NEXT SESSION.

QUESTIONS:

1. Your first tool for witnessing is a clear forceful personal testimony?
(T) or (F)

2. In your Testimony, you should always avoid Christian clichés that are meaningless to a Non-Christian. (T) or (F)

3 When you give a personal testimony, the emphasis should be placed on what must be given up to receive eternal life? (T) or (F)

4. To have an effective testimony, it is good to have specific events and examples because people forget generalities. (T) or (F)

5. You can witness effectively even when you are not sure that you have Eternal Life. (T) or (F)

6. A testimony used during the Start Fresh Introduction should clearly tell how to receive eternal life (T) or (F)

7. The purpose of the church is to show the reality of eternal life and to share the message of eternal life. (T) or (F)

8. Over past History, the church has done a poor job of communicating the message of eternal life. (T) or (F)

9 When do we share our testimony? _Every Opportunity_

10 If you don't have a testimony, you might have a ___SiN___ problem.

11 A personal testimony _____ a desire to hear the gospel

12 When you give your testimony in the introduction, be careful not to give the answer to why you came to know Jesus Christ. (T) or (F)

13 The main focus of your personal testimony is not about our _____, but God's _____.

14 Do you adapt your testimony to your prospects' needs. (T) or (F)

15 Before you get into the Start Fresh Presentation, when you get to the end of your testimony always ask may I ask you a question. (T) or (F)

SESSION #3

START FRESH GOSPEL

INTRODUCTION

SESSION #3

Gospel Introduction

1. **Talk about something in common**
   A. **Their work**
   B. **Their neighborhood**
   C. **Their House**
   D. **Their Church Background**

Transfer into the Gospel by asking them a question

Q1.   Ever wish you could wipe away the slate clean and start over?

Q2.   Have you thought about that if you died today, would you go to heaven?

If they answer with "Yes" to the second question, you ask why do you say yes? If they say they are a Christian, read the Bible, go to church, pray every night, Muslim, Buddhist, Jehovah Witness, etc. then proceed with the Gospel!!!

   E. **Present the Gospel to them. Remember, the power is in the Gospel. You are letting God's Word touch their hearts.**

TRANSITION INTO THE GOSPEL

CAN I TELL YOU SOMETHING THAT I JUST HEARD? IT USES THE ACCROSTIC OF THE WORD "START"

The Gospel Is Good News

The word Gospel, as used in the New Testament, means "a good message" or "to announce good news."

For our task of Evangelism, leading others into relationship with Jesus, we must determine what this good news could be.

Gospel vs. Gospels

Just so we are not confused, there is a difference between the above mentioned terms. The "Gospel" is the message that we are going to learn about here and present to people who need a relationship with Jesus.

The "Gospels" are what we call the first four books of the New Testament; Matthew, Mark, Luke and John. These four books chronicle Jesus' birth, life on earth, death and resurrection.

"Teaching them to observe all things that I have commanded you."
Matthew 28:20

In reality, all of what Jesus taught that is recorded in the four Gospels is part of the Good News. It is why they are called THE GOSPELS! Everything in God's Word is good news to those who will believe it and live according to it.

The people who lived during New Testament times were looking for a Messiah, a Savior, who had been told about by the prophets of Old Testament times. The good news for them was that He had arrived.

There should have been great rejoicing over Jesus' coming, but some doubted and would not believe the good news.

The Gospel - A Summary

Part 1 -   S -   (God loves us and wants an eternal relationship with us) So we need to **STOP making excuses for your sin**.

Part 2 -   T -   (Man disobeyed and fell away from intimate relationship with God) **TAKE a look at your past – does it honor God?**

Part 3 -   A -   (God has a plan to get us back into a right relationship that involves Sacrifice. **ACTION speaks louder than words)**

Part 4 -   R-   (Jesus makes the sacrifice for us) **If your life becomes blurry, REFOCUS your life**

Part 5 -   T-   (We only need to accept Jesus' sacrifice and repent (turn away) from our disobedience (sin) in order to come back into right relationship with God. **Who are you going to TRUST**.

Tip #1

As you begin to share the good news with people, you will soon realize that each person is at a different level of understanding and will need a different starting point in the outline with the message of the Gospel.

This book is designed to give you a complete overview of: God's Love, why do we need Salvation, how Jesus offers us that Salvation and what we need to do in order to receive His Salvation. So, let the Holy Spirit guide you in where you need to begin to share with each individual. Each part of the message builds on the other with the start fresh outline.

Here Is The Really Good News!

Because Jesus made the sacrifice for us, there is a way for us to come into right relationship with God!

Jesus said, "I am the way, the truth and the life; no man comes to the Father but by me." *John 14:6*

Jesus' sacrifice on the cross opens a door for our access into the Kingdom of God. So, what do we need to do in order to go through that door.

"Repent (turn away from your sin) and be baptized every one of you in the name of Jesus Christ for the remission (forgiveness) of sins, and you will receive the gift of the Holy Ghost." *Acts 2:38*

This was the Apostle Peter's reply to the people when they asked, "What shall we do?"

Tip #2

Many people try to begin witnessing to others with the part of the message that includes repentance. Many people want to get to the finish line before they even start. Many people don't understand the idea of repentance or turning away from sin because they have no concept of what sin is. At times, you will need a way to take a non-believer through all five parts of the outline in order for them to understand their need for a relationship with God. Become familiar with the reason "why" we need salvation. Build on a solid foundation. Sometimes you have to begin with "S" (Stop making excuses for sin) before you can get to the "T" (Trust).

Many people have come to know the Lord through a series of Scriptures in the book of Romans. Commonly called, "**The Roman Road to Salvation**" these Scriptures give a quick reference outline to the Gospel message.

Romans 3:23 - "For all have sinned and come short of the glory of God..." Establishes the fact that we are **ALL** sinners who are separated from God.

Romans 3:10: *"As it is written: There is no one righteous, not even one."* No one can earn right standing with God. We must understand that our good deeds or religion are unacceptable to God because our good works cannot cancel out our sin. For a view of man's sinful condition,

Romans 5:8 - "God demonstrates His own love toward us, in that while we were still sinners, Christ died for us." Again, we are shown the sacrifice made on our behalf, illustrating God's great love for us and His desire to be with us for the rest of eternity.

Romans 6:23 - "For the wages of sin is death; but the gift of God is eternal life through Jesus Christ our Lord."

Romans 8:1: *"Therefore, there is now no condemnation for those who are in Christ Jesus."* By accepting Jesus' death as a payment for our sins, we will never be condemned for our sins.

Romans 10:13 - "Whoever calls on the name of the Lord will be saved." Repentance, submitting, following the teaching of Jesus Christ is required for salvation. Saved from what? Saved from an eternity separated from God. Saved to what? Saved to an eternal home in heaven, described in Revelation 21:1-7

Romans 10:9-10: *"That if you confess with your mouth, "Jesus is Lord," and believe in your heart that God raised him from the dead, you will be saved. For it is with your heart that you believe and are justified, and it is with your mouth that you confess and are saved."* We must believe that the Lord Jesus Christ is the Son of God Who died for us on the cross, rose from the dead, and is Lord. We must put our trust in Jesus alone to make us right with God. Salvation involves believing in our hearts (inward belief) and an outward confession that Jesus is Lord.

Romans 10:13: *"For everyone who calls on the name of the Lord will be saved."* There is no complicated formula to salvation; Jesus paid the price of our sin for us. Our response is to accept Jesus as our Lord and Savior. If we do, we will be saved from eternal death in Hell to eternal life in Heaven.

Revelation20:10-15. God gives us a gift that we do not deserve through the sacrifice of Jesus Christ.

Or by other programs through outlines of scriptures. **So why do we need to share?**

Matthew 24:14- And this gospel of the kingdom will be preached in all the world as a witness to all the nations, and then the end will come.

Mark 16:15- And He said to them, "Go into all the world and preach the gospel to every creature.

Mark 13:10- And the gospel must first be preached to all the nations.

Most people today would answer that question by saying "No" only qualified people should share or they give so many excuses not to share. Like:

A. I might push people away.
B. I might lose my friends.
C. I might lose my job.
D. I do it by living the Gospel rather than telling others about the Gospel
E. I don't know many unbelievers.
F. It's not my calling.
G. I don't know how to tell the Gospel.

The bible tells us that every believer should "GO" and "TELL"

1 Peter 2:9-10   But you *are* a chosen generation, a royal priesthood, a holy nation, His own special people, that you may proclaim the praises of Him who called you out of darkness into His marvelous light; who once *were* not a people but *are* now the people of God, who had not obtained mercy but now have obtained mercy.

This scripture shows us that the people of God, collectively, are a chosen race, a royal priesthood, a holy nation, and His own special people. This is modeled by Peter, who has essentially only spoken of the Gospel to this point in his letter. As such, every Christian should understand that Matthew 28 and Acts 1 commissions to apply to all people.

All believers should be concerned with sharing the Gospel not only to the lost and dying world. We should share it from across the street, into the city, to the state, to the nation and across the seas.

The Gospel should be a frequent topic of conversation for all who know Jesus. Why *would* we not and how *can* we not proclaim Him who has called us out of darkness and into His marvelous light?

SESSION #3 B

Introduction

Who Needs to Be Visited:

Anyone needing encouragement, comfort, or a sense of belonging would profit from a visit. New Church visitors need a visit soon after they have visited your church. Neighborhoods around your church need visits. Just pick a street. While that could include everyone, there are certain individuals who especially need to be reminded that they aren't forgotten. These are people who can feel rather lonely at times.

- Prisoners

- People in shelters

- Elderly people still living independently especially if they are shut-ins

- Elderly or disabled people living in nursing homes

- People who are sick for a prolonged period of time

- People who are hospitalized

- Bereaved people

- People in crisis

We could add to the list those who are unsaved who may be reached through door-to-door visitation. Visitation to the unsaved and to visitors would fall more under this outreach.

Can Anyone Do The Visitation?:

Many pastors get a lot of criticism for failure to go do visitation. Realistically, however, if the pastor is to adequately prepare sermons, do counseling, provide general leadership for the church staff. There is Little time to make many visits. Some churches may hire a visitation/ outreach pastor to bridge the gap. Some churches have a visitation team to share the load.

When you look at the passages of Scripture, is that visitation is a corporate effort not just the pastor's or committee's job. If we are truly going to express care for one another, then we must sometimes go where the people are. We must lay aside our busy schedules and excuses and make people a priority.

How nice it is if one of the pastors from the church visits in our time of need. How encouraging if another member also visits during this time of crisis. But to have numerous people visit over the course of time, now there's a caring church.

What Should Happen in a Typical Visit?

It is common to have a fear of not knowing what to say or do is one of the big stumbling blocks to going out on visitation. You don't have to have a planned program to visit someone. **Just being there matters more to them than what you do or say.** Your presence communicates that you care and that is the bottom line in visiting someone in need. If you go with an obvious agenda, or planned out speech, people could feel that your agenda matters more than they do. Let the Holy Spirit lead you through the visit.

If one of the team members can easily get you in the door, then choose before you leave the church who is going to start the conversation. Also make sure you know who will start to share the Gospel, then the other team members will pray silently and participate when needed. Always work as a team.

Here are some tips:

1. Extend the gift of touch. Smile, shake hands and be friendly.

2. Spend most of your time listening. Asking questions at appropriate time.

3. Remember that you are there for them and not for yourself so be respectful.

4. Be sensitive with what you do say

5. Offer to pray with or for them.

6. Leave something with them as a reminder of your visit like a Church card, a flower, music, a book, last week's bulletin, or any small token.

There may be some dangers or compromising situations that you can avoid by not going out alone. Have evangelism partners with you. Preferably 2 men and a women or 2 women and a man.

Have a Set Time To Go

It is important to be a soul winner all week, but it is also important to have a designated time sanctified solely to the cause of trying to share the gospel. Jesus implied this truth of going and preaching in:

Matthew 11:1 "And it came to pass, when Jesus had made an end of commanding his twelve disciples, he departed thence to teach and to preach in their cities."

Mark 1:38 "And he said unto them, Let us go into the next towns, that I may preach there also: for therefore came I forth."

Mark 3:14 "And he ordained twelve, that they should be with him, and that he might send them forth to preach,"

Luke 9:2 "And he sent them to preach the kingdom of God, and to heal the sick."

Before Leaving- Start Out With Prayer

Pray for power, wisdom, boldness, safety and for the people you see to be saved.

Where to Go:

1. New Visitors of the church
2. Door to Door (just pick a street and start knocking!)
3. Connection Group or Sunday School visitors
4. Hospitals
5. Parks or Downtown
6. New church attenders
7. People who haven't been to church or Sunday School in a while
8. The Whole World! Just "GO"

Watch Out For "Fellowship"

James 3:10 "Out of the same mouth proceedeth blessing and cursing. My brethren, these things ought not so to be."

While with your evangelism partners, resist the temptation to say negative things about other people or the church. Keep your focus on souls. Do not gossip, slander, backbite, or whisper.

Leave your problems at home. This is not a time to dump your problems on your partners, this is time to rescue the perishing. **The worst day in a believer's life is better than the best day in a lost person's eternity**.

Only speak what is good for edifying. Talk about your soul winning and how you can improve. Keep your mind and passion on the lost. Think of hell, and how you might be the only one who will ever cross paths with these people.

Be Prepared – What To Take with you in the car:

1. Carry a Small New Testament Bible

Carry a New Testament, not a full-size Bible. Try to conceal it, perhaps in your back pocket or your purse, like you'd carry a wallet. It is best not to have anything in your hands unless you are carrying flyers for a special event coming up at your church. If people see something in your hand, they may think you are a salesman and will take a defensive posture. If they see a Bible, they may think you are a religious nut.

2. Tracts

Carry good gospel tracts in your shirt pocket. If they are old, bent, soiled, or folded, throw them out. We live in a day when "packaging" and "image" means everything. We must pass out nice gospel tracts. They are inexpensive, so only give out ones in good condition.

3. Paper for notes (perhaps 3x5 cards) (prayer request or a note for the door)

4. Pen or Pencil

5. Breath mints

Watch your breath – Presume it is bad! (LOL)

6. Addresses of visits and an appropriate map page to help save time not getting lost.

7. A Visitation sheet on the prospect to hand in to the Visitation director. This sheet is at the end of this training book and can be copied.

All Teams going out will need to have a Plan

Decide ahead of time who will be the "silent partner" (this will be discussed more later) and who will speak. If you have an idea of who you will be visiting, discuss what may be expected and how to handle various problems.

I. Approaching the House

Be careful where you park your car or walk. Do not park or walk over grass. Use sidewalks or driveways to walk up to the door. Often you'll find that the yard and driveway are very important to people. Be considerate of these. If in a neighborhood, park on the street if safety permits. We do not want to block the driveway. If your car leaks oil or fluids, park by the road and walk up to the house.

Approaching the Door

A Communication Problem For Sure!
An energetic new church member knocked on the door, and, when the man of the house answered, the well-meaning witness asked "Are there any Christians here?"
"No," responded the man. We're the Joneses." "I mean, are you lost?"
"Oh, no, we've lived here 25 years and know the area very well."
"Well...," the new church member asked, "where will you be on Judgment Day?" "I don't know. What day is it?"
"Well, we don't really know. It could be one day or another."
"Be sure to let us know," "I'm sure my wife will want to go both days."

Communicating our faith can often be a frustrating and a defeating problem. Often, we hear sermons on the urgency of witnessing, but when we go out to try it, we leave feeling not only fruitless, but also confused and anxious. **How do we get started? What do we talk about?** Words seem to come hard, and thoughts often cannot filter through our fears.

6 Things to look at while going door to door.

A. Be Observant

Some people live in fear. If a sign says, "No trespassing;" "Trespassers will be shot;" "Guard Dogs on Duty;" or "No Solicitors," beware. You might accomplish more if you call ahead or note the address and send a card with a gospel tract in it. The respect you show for these people's wishes might touch their hearts.

"Beware of Dogs..." **Philippians 3:2**. I have been bit twice while out on visitation. If you feel there is a real danger of physical harm, again, it might be better for you to write down the address and send them a note with a tract inside.

B. Use Common Sense

If someone is mowing their lawn, they probably do not want to be disturbed. If there is a big party going on it would be a better testimony to go back another day. Use some old fashioned common sense.

Note the "not-homes" and go back another time, maybe on a different day or at a different time. After you've gone back two or three times, leave a note and a tract. Don't give up after only one try!

C. Do Not Talk When Approaching a House

Avoid making comments about the yard or house until you engage them in conversation. Never say anything like, "They ought to fix this rain gutter" or "They could use some paint on this house" or "They must have kids." It is best to say nothing until they answer the door.

D. Step Back From the Door

After knocking, take a few steps back. If there are stairs, step down one or two. Give them space! The space will give them some peace and show them that you are non-threatening. Make sure that you have a nametag with your name and church name. Only approach them after you have introduced yourself to shake their hand, or enter their house if they let you in.

E. Look Away From the Door

Knock on the door and look away. Let them open the door and see you first. It is scary to have unknown people staring at you!

F. Smile

Put a smile on your face. There is a lot of power in a smile and friendliness. Try to win them to yourself, it will help you win them to the Lord.

WHAT DO YOU SAY???

What do you say when someone answers the door? Here are two scenarios:

A. Door-to-Door

Begin by introducing yourself:

"Hi, my name is Bo and this is Mike and Anita. We're from _____ Church and we're out meeting our neighbors and wanted to stop by and say 'hi.' We were trying to get to know more people in the area. What is your name?"

Then remember their name! Sometimes we are concentrating so much on what we should say next, we do not pay attention to what they are saying. Relax! Be friendly, be human, be real. Avoid a "canned-presentation." Be yourself.

Try to Win them to yourself so you can win them to Christ. Jesus was very personal and friendly with people. He was known as the "Friend of Publicans and Sinners."

Find a comfortable way to "break the ice." Compliment them or seriously inquire about them. For example:

"Have you lived here a long time?"
"Where are you from originally?" (If they just moved in).
"How many children do you have?" (If there are children around).
"What do you do for a living?"
""You have a beautiful home!

People love to talk about themselves, their children, their interests, their house, their employment. They do not like to talk about politics, religion, or money ("How much did this house cost?" "What are your car payments?" and "How much do you earn?" are no-no's.)

Eventually turn the conversation around to the condition of their souls. This can be done quite effectively by asking them if they have a church home and inviting them to the church services. If you hand them the tract showing them the church schedule, you can say, "We would be honored to have you as a guest at our church sometime. Here's a leaflet with the schedule of our services on it." They will invariably look on the inside and cover of the tract. You can then say, "before we go may I ask you a question? I had someone ask me if I could wipe the slate clean and start over would I want to do that? The bible says I write these things to you that you may know that you have eternal life. May I ask you another question? Have you thought about if you died today would you go to heaven?

They will probably respond, "I sure hope so" or "I think so."

You can then answer with something like, "Sir, for some time in my life I didn't know either. I thought you had to wait and find out. Then someone shared with me how I could know that I'm going to heaven. God loves us and wants us to be able to know now."

At this point you can then go into the Start Fresh outline. Don't wait for his permission. He'll stop you if he doesn't want to hear it.

We will discuss the gospel presentation in the next section.

B. Visiting a Contact

Perhaps you are going to visit a home that has already had contact with our church either by visit, attending or by email or phone call:

You could start by saying, "We're Bo, Anita and Mike from (state your church name), and we wanted to stop by on behalf of the church and say 'Thank you' for visiting our church."

They will probably respond some way. I really liked it. Then, while handing them a tract with a church connection group (Sunday School) schedule on and inviting them to come back to be a part of our growing church. (make the invitation inviting)

Again, by turning her attention to the inside of the tract you might be able to start sharing the gospel with him/ her.

Conversation should be friendly and can take many different twists. Feel free to spend a little time with the person, but once you have started the gospel presentation, **stick to the subject**.

If they bring up doctrinal questions or questions about religions, you could say something like: "That's a good question and I think I might be able to give you a good answer, but just so I don't lose my train of thought, let me finish explaining this to you." If you try to answer their question during the gospel presentation, you might start a contention and get derailed. Stick to the subject. Let them talk, but control the conversation.

Another ice-breaking question is, "Mrs. Johnson, is there any particular church you attend regularly?" By her answer you can often find out her spiritual standing. If she names a particular church you know of, you might want to complement their building or grounds. Don't give the impression that you approve of their religion, however.

Then you could respond by saying "I'm glad to meet someone who has some interest in spiritual things. Mrs. Johnson, have you thought about if you were to die you would go to heaven?" Then lead into a gospel presentation.

These two examples are your basic soul-winning opportunities in church-wide visitation: Door-to-door and visiting contacts.

SESSION #3C

QUESTIONS:

1. During the introduction part of the visit. Does it give you the right to ask him/her the questions to the gospel? (T) or (F)

2. At the time of the introduction, the mood setting needs to be (somewhat light) or (more relaxed)

3. When you pull up to a home, how long do you stay in the car? (2 min.) (5 min.) (get out as soon as you get there)

4. In the introduction time, the witness will try to do:
   a. be quiet and _____ to earn the right to be heard
   b. _____ things in their home and give a sincere _____.
   c. That we can _____ _____ that move from their life to the gospel.

5. When walking up to the house. It is good to carry a large print full Bible   (T) or (F)

6. If the Gospel is rejected, do you make your exit quick, or try to convince them to not reject the gospel. _____

7. Do you criticize a person's denomination, pastor or congregation? _____

8. When we discuss our personal testimony, we should show our change That came as a result of receiving eternal life? (T) or (F)

9. Because you are visiting from the church, it's natural to talk about their church background. (T) or (F)

10. Is it good to tell the prospect that they are wrong in their views? (T) or (F)

DOOR TO DOOR VISITATION

DOOR TO DOOR TRAINING STARTS AT WEEK 3

TRAINEE SHOULD PARTICIPATE WITH THE INTRODUCTION OF THE OUTLINE

Gospel Introduction

    Talk about something in common
        Their work
        Their neighborhood
        Their House
        Their Church Background

Transfer into the Gospel by asking them a question

Q1. Ever wish you could wipe away the slate clean and start over?

Q2. Have you thought about that if you died today, would you go to heaven?

Trainees can do their Testimony during this visit.

SESSION #4

START FRESH

GOSPEL

OUTLINE

"S"– Stop Making Excuses For Your Sin

"T" -Take A Look At My Past – Did It Honor God?

"A" – Actions Speak Louder Than Words

"R" – If Life Gets Blurry – Refocus Your Life

"T" – Who Are You Going To Trust?

SESSION #4

The Gospel Presentation

Your team partners should be nice, friendly, and engaging in conversation. But once the gospel presentation begins, the team should stop talking and become the silent partners. So Decide ahead of time which role you will play.

The silent partners should look at the person as he or she is sharing the gospel (do not stare at the one being talked to). The team should also silently pray for the Word of God to affect the lost soul, and for that soul's salvation. The silent partners should also run interference to make sure that nothing (pets, kids, other people, etc.) distracts the soul from hearing the gospel.

The easiest way for the "talking partners" to share the gospel is by simply a conversation with the person. Not to make it a memorized script. Have with you Start Fresh tracts available.

A. In These Last Days of Uncertainty, Here's One Thing You Can Know For Sure

Do you know for sure that you will go to heaven someday? God wrote the Bible so that you can know! **I John 5:13** says, "These things have I written unto you ... that ye may KNOW that ye have Eternal Life."

Here's how you can know:

1. We must realize that we've all sinned. **Romans 3:23** says "For all have sinned, and come short of the glory of God."

2. The penalty for our sins is death and eternal separation from God. The Bible says in **Romans 6:23**: "For the wages of sin is death." **Ezekiel 18:20** says, "The soul that sinneth, it shall die." (See **Revelation 20:14; 21:8** as well).

3. Jesus paid our death penalty for us. God sent Jesus to suffer and die in our place on the Cross. **Romans 5:8** says, "But God commendeth [showed] His love toward us, in that, while we were yet sinners, Christ died for us." He was buried and rose from the grave and is alive forevermore!

4. God loves you and wants to save you from your sins. "For God so loved the world, that He gave His only begotten Son, that whosoever believeth in Him should not perish, but have everlasting life." **John 3:16.**

However, each person must accept Christ personally to be saved from their own sins. Jesus said, "I am the way, the truth, and the life: no man cometh unto the Father, but by me**," John 14:6**. "Neither is there salvation in any other: for there is none other name under heaven given among men, whereby we must be saved," **Acts 4:12.**

There is no other way. Salvation is not through being good, doing works, keeping a moral code, being religious or any other efforts of our own. Salvation is only through the Lord Jesus Christ and His finished work on Calvary's Cross. Only His shed blood can wash away our sins. (See **Romans 5:9; Ephesians 1:7**)

How can you accept Christ as your Savior? Romans 10:13 tells us, "For whosoever shall call upon the Name of the Lord shall be saved." John 1:12 says, "But as many as received Him, to them gave He power to become the sons of God, even to them that believe on His Name."

Pray, believing from your heart, "Lord I admit that I am a sinner and deserve Your punishment in hell. Forgive me for my sins - I repent. I now trust Jesus Christ as my personal Savior and call upon Him to save me from my sins. I believe that He died for me on the Cross and only His blood can wash away my sins. I ask for Your gift of Eternal Life, in Jesus Name, Amen!"

"...the gift of God is eternal life through Jesus Christ our Lord." **Romans 6:23b**

B. If You Were to Die Today, Are You 100% Sure that You Would Go to Heaven?

There are just 4 things you need to know in order to go to Heaven for sure:

1. You need to know that you are a sinner.

The Bible says in **Romans 3:23**, "For all have sinned and come short of the glory of God."

2. You need to know that there is a penalty for that sin - Death.

The Bible says in **Romans 6:23a**, "For the wages of sin is death..."

This word "death" doesn't mean just dying and going to the grave. It means separation from God forever and ever in a lake of fire. This is our punishment for our sin and a debt you owe as of right now.

3. You need to know that Jesus loves you so much that He paid that penalty for you by shedding His blood on the cross for your sins.

The Bible says in **Romans 5:8-9** "But God commendeth his love toward us, in that, while we were yet sinners, Christ died for us. Much more then, being now justified by his blood, we shall be saved from wrath through him."

4. You need to know that Jesus offers you the free gift of Heaven.

The Bible says in **Romans 6:23b**, "... But the gift of God is eternal life through Jesus Christ our Lord."

Going to Heaven is a gift. It's absolutely free! You can't buy it, work for it, go to church for it, or be good for it. Its absolutely free! Ephesians 2:8-9, "For by grace are ye saved through faith; and that not of yourselves: it is the gift of God: Not of works, lest any man should boast."
In review: You know you are a sinner. You realize there is a penalty for that sin and you can't pay for it yourself;

You believe Jesus died on the cross and shed His blood for your sins. You can to accept God's free gift of eternal life for you through Jesus Christ our Lord.

STOP MAKING EXCUSES FOR

YOUR SIN

SESSION #4A

S - STOP MAKING EXCUSES FOR YOUR SIN

I keep wondering why we so often attempt to make excuses for sins in our lives. How is that though we say we love God, so often it is difficult to look at ourselves head-on and see the sin that God sees? How come it is so easy to make excuses to others, who often see us for what we are, and the sins we commit? Why is it that the sins we try to hide the most, are the ones that keep coming to light, until we finally say, "No more excuses"?

Some other "pet" excuses used by people are "it's my personality" or "God made me that way." I have to smile at these in a way, because I've heard those same excuses used by people that abhor psychology and the "personality" breakdowns. Many would recognize that referring to the "four personalities" as an excuse for behaving ungodly is sin. In fact, regardless of how unique God has made each of us, the Bible clearly states that all are to have evidence of the fruit of the Spirit. There are no verses that describe or let us make excuses for sin because of our personalities, backgrounds or circumstances. But there are many verses that say we are to change and put off sin. God expects that of us.

We can often deceive ourselves with our excuses, and justify remaining in sin and committing more sins. This type of behavior

Can happen over and over. It depends on how sensitive we are to the leading of the Holy Spirit. As well, justifying and deceiving ourselves can make us believe that we are absolutely right in our behavior, and that thinking often leads to further sin.

Jeremiah 17:9 " The heart is deceitful above all things, and desperately wicked: who can know it?"

This is what happened to me one night at the Jail when I was teaching this same outline and 8 men came to know Christ. I was walking down the hallway and God said to write it. I was arguing with God, giving all kinds of excuses. He always came back with an answer. That is where this book came alive.

"Who Me?" "Why Me Lord?"

Moses gives God five of the weakest excuses ever. Yet God was not willing to take "no" for an answer from those whom He calls, he comes back with a response every time. I'm sure Moses was not too happy.

First Excuse

Moses: "But God, I couldn't possibly do what you ask me to do. I have no experience in the negotiation business." (**Exodus 3:11**) And Moses said unto

 God, Who am I, that I should go unto Pharaoh, and that I should bring forth the children of Israel out of Egypt?

God: "I'll go with you and tell you what to say." (**Exodus 3:12**) And he said, Certainly I will be with thee; and this shall be a token unto thee, that I have sent thee: When thou hast brought forth the people out of Egypt, ye shall serve God upon this mountain.

Second Excuse

Moses: "I don't want them to get mad at me so who should I say sent me?" (**Exodus 3:13**) And Moses said unto God, Behold, when I come unto the children of Israel, and shall say unto them, The God of your fathers hath sent me unto you; and they shall say to me, What is his name? what shall I say unto them?
God: "Don't worry, Moses, they know who I AM."
(**Exodus 3:14-15**) And God said unto Moses, I AM THAT I AM: and he said, Thus shalt thou say unto the children of Israel, I AM hath sent me unto you. And God said moreover unto Moses, Thus shalt thou say unto the children of Israel, The LORD God of your fathers, the God of Abraham, the God of Isaac, and the God of Jacob, hath sent me unto you: this is my name for ever, and this is my memorial unto all generations.

Third Excuse

Moses: "What if they don't believe me?"
(**Exodus 4:1**) And Moses answered and said, But, behold, they will not believe me, nor hearken unto my voice: for they will say, The LORD hath not appeared unto thee.
God: "Don't worry about that, I've got your back. They love signs. I'll give them signs."
(**Exodus 4:2-9**) And the LORD said unto him, What is that in thine hand? And he said, A rod. And he said, Cast it on the ground. And he cast it on the ground, and it became a serpent; and Moses fled from before it. And the LORD

said unto Moses, Put forth thine hand, and take it by the tail. And he put forth his hand, and caught it, and it became a rod in his hand: That they may believe that the LORD God of their fathers, the God of Abraham, the God of Isaac, and the God of Jacob, hath appeared unto thee. And the LORD said furthermore unto him, Put now thine hand into thy bosom. And he put his hand into his bosom: and when he took it out, behold, his hand was leprous as snow. And he said, Put thine hand into thy bosom again. And he put his hand into his bosom again; and plucked it out of his bosom, and, behold, it was turned again as his other flesh. And it shall come to pass, if they will not believe thee, neither hearken to the voice of the first sign, that they will believe the voice of the latter sign. And it shall come to pass, if they will not believe also these two signs, neither hearken unto thy voice, that thou shalt take of the water of the river, and pour it upon the dry land: and the water which thou takest out of the river shall become blood upon the dry land.

Fourth Excuse

Moses: "But Lord, Who's going to listen to me to a man who stutters?"
(Exodus 4:10) And Moses said unto the LORD, O my Lord, I am not eloquent, neither heretofore, nor since thou hast spoken unto thy servant: but I am slow of speech, and of a slow tongue.
God: "I made your tongue and I can make you speak to be understood."
(Exodus 4:11-12) And the LORD said unto him, Who hath made man's mouth? or who maketh the dumb, or deaf, or the seeing, or the blind? have not I the LORD? Now therefore go, and I will be with thy mouth, and teach thee what thou shalt say.

Fifth Excuse

Moses: "I hate to bring this up Lord, but I killed a man and I don't think I am the man for the job. Can't you find someone else?"
(Exodus 4:13) And he said, O my Lord, send, I pray thee, by the hand of him whom thou wilt send.
God: "I don't want anyone else. You're just the man for the job. You used to be a somebody. You were a prince of Egypt. I couldn't use you then. Now you're a nobody. I specialize in nobodies. Now I can use you." And the anger of the LORD was kindled against Moses, and he said, Is not Aaron the Levite thy brother? I know that he can speak well. And also, behold, he cometh forth to meet thee: and when he seeth thee, he will be glad in his heart. And thou shalt speak unto him, and put words in his mouth: and I will be with thy mouth, and with his mouth, and will teach you what ye shall do. And he shall be thy spokesman unto the people: and he shall be, even he shall be to thee instead of a mouth, and thou shalt be to him instead of God.

STOP MAKING EXCUSES
FOR
YOUR SIN!!!

SESSION #4B

What is your excuse?

A. For not stepping out of the boat by faith?

Romans 14:23- But he who doubts is condemned if he eats, because *he does* not *eat* from faith; for whatever *is* not from faith is sin.

B. For not doing something for God?

Luke 21:14- Whom shall I send and who will go? Excuses, excuses, excuses, what are yours?

C. For not reading your bible?

2 Timothy 2:15- Study to show thyself approved unto God, a workman that needeth not to be ashamed, rightly dividing the word of truth.

D. For not praying?

1 Thessalonians 5:18- In every thing give thanks: for this is the will of God in Christ Jesus concerning you.

E. For not going to church faithfully?

Hebrews 10:25- Not forsaking the assembling of ourselves together, as the manner of some is; but exhorting one another: and so much the more, as ye see the day approaching.

F. For not telling people about Jesus Christ?

Acts 20:20- And how I kept back nothing that was profitable unto you, but have showed you, and have taught you publicly, and from house to house,

G. For not surrendering everything to God?

Matthew 19:29- "And every one that hath forsaken houses, or brethren, or sisters, or father, or mother, or wife, or children, or lands, for my name's sake, shall receive an hundredfold, and shall inherit everlasting life."

Romans 2:1

Therefore you have no excuse, O man, every one of you who judges. For in passing judgment on another you condemn yourself, because you, the judge, practice the very same things.

Romans 1:20

For his invisible attributes, namely, his eternal power and divine nature, have been clearly perceived, ever since the creation of the world, in the things that have been made. So they are without excuse.

John 15:22

If I had not come and spoken to them, they would not have been guilty of sin, but now they have no excuse for their sin.

Romans 2:1-29

Therefore you have no excuse, O man, every one of you who judges. For in passing judgment on another you condemn yourself, because you, the judge, practice the very same things. We know that the judgment of God rightly falls on those who practice such things. Do you suppose, O man—you who judge those who practice such things and yet do them yourself—that you will escape the judgment of God? Or do you presume on the riches of his kindness and forbearance and patience, not knowing that God's kindness is meant to lead you to repentance? But because of your hard and impenitent heart you are storing up wrath for yourself on the day of wrath when God's righteous judgment will be revealed. ...

Matthew 7:21

"Not everyone who says to me, 'Lord, Lord,' will enter the kingdom of heaven, but the one who does the will of my Father who is in heaven.

2 Peter 3:9

The Lord is not slow to fulfill his promise as some count slowness, but is patient toward you, not wishing that any should perish, but that all should reach repentance.

Romans 6:23

For the wages of sin is death, but the free gift of God is eternal life in Christ Jesus our Lord.

John 3:16

"For God so loved the world, that he gave his only Son, that whoever believes in him should not perish but have eternal life.

1 John 1:9

If we confess our sins, he is faithful and just to forgive us our sins and to cleanse us from all unrighteousness.

James 4:17

So whoever knows the right thing to do and fails to do it, for him it is sin.

Hebrews 10:26

For if we go on sinning deliberately after receiving the knowledge of the truth, there no longer remains a sacrifice for sins,

2 Corinthians 5:17

Therefore, if anyone is in Christ, he is a new creation. The old has passed away; behold, the new has come.

Why do some people say drinking "one beer" or "one glass of wine" is ok with God? It's not ok with God. Wine and strong drink is a mockery to God. God said so in Proverbs. Why do some people say a little lie is not going to matter. They're deceived by sin.

They haven't studied the Bible closely nor do they want to because it "exposes" their excuse to sinful conduct. Why do people fornicate today and ask God to forgive them tonight and then fornicate over again tomorrow or next week? Sin has dominion over their conscience and character. They are actually a slave to sin and in their conscience they will excuse sinful living.

Why do some people excuse sin? Their mind and intellect is darkened by the nature of the fall and they have a "self justification" to make every excuse known to man. Excuse after excuse, "Who are they really kidding?"

Not God! People excuse sin in their own intellect and in their own reasoning. Excuses made for sin will not take you to Heaven.

Sin is brought to light when Christ truly takes you over. There will be no more excuses to sin because you will realize the magnitude of a clean heart made you personally clean by the death of a Savior on the cross. Each individual believer actually gets to Christ on a personal level. A personal clean heart! Glory! Then sin is forgiven, realized, and thus uprooted in your life! No more excuses to sin, but inclination to live holy and right! The person, the power, and the presence of Christ shows this believer how to live, how to act and, how to behave. Realization of Christ brings accountability to you which in turn shows you, the right way to go.

You will not excuse sin when Christ takes you over completely...You will not blame the Devil when Christ takes you over completely.

Making Excuses For Your Sin

Proverbs 28:13- He that covers his sins will not prosper,
but whoever confesses and forsakes them will have mercy.

If we face our problems and properly deal with them, we can have God's Mercy.

During the storms in our lives, we want to stop trying and give up. We push God away instead of bringing Him closer. We need to STOP making excuses, admit it when it is our responsibility and move on.

SESSION #4C

QUESTIONS:

1. If I want a fresh start in life, I have to stop making **excuses** for my failures.

2. I've got to stop _____ other people. I've got to stop seeing myself as the **victim** of my circumstances. Other people can hurt us, other people can harm us, and other people can scar us. But the only person that can ruin your life is **you**. Nobody can ruin your life without your permission. You have a choice and that is you can choose how you're going to respond to those hurts. The Bible says that the starting point is to just be honest and accept responsibility for my part in the problem.

3. **Proverbs 28:13-** He who _____ his sins will not prosper, But whoever _____ and forsakes *them* will have mercy.

4. **Proverbs 20:7-** The righteous *man* _____ in his integrity; His children *are* blessed after him.

5. **Isaiah 43:18**- Do not _____ the former things, Nor consider the things of old.

6. If we face our problems and properly deal with them, we can have God's mercy. **(T) or (F)**

7. What are some typical excuses that you hear people make?
   _____

8. Why do they make those excuses? Then honestly evaluate yourself, do you make the same or similar excuses?
   _____

9. How is it that sin is so deceptive that we do not even notice when it is alive and well in our being?
   _____

10 Why do we cover our sins? _____

DOOR TO DOOR VISITATION

DOOR TO DOOR TRAINING WEEK 4

TRAINEE SHOULD PARTICIPATE WITH THE INTRODUCTION OF THE OUTLINE

Gospel Introduction

Talk about something in common
Their work
Their neighborhood
Their House
Their Church Background

Transfer into the Gospel by asking them a question

Q1. **Ever wish you could wipe away the slate clean and start over?**

Q2. **Have you thought about that if you died today, would you go to heaven?**

Trainees can do their Testimony during this visit.

"S" – STOP MAKING EXCUSES FOR YOUR SIN

SESSION #5

IF YOU KEEP ON REPEATING THE CHAPTERS, YOUR ENDING WILL NEVER CHANGE

CHANGE NOTHING AND NOTHING CHANGES!!!!

SESSION #5

T - TAKE A LOOK AT YOUR PAST – DID IT HONOR GOD

I need to take an inventory of my life. That means I need to evaluate all my experiences. I   need to look at what I have left after the failure. I need to take an inventory of my life's experiences and learn from them.
Galatians 3:3-5- Are you so foolish? Having begun in the Spirit, are you now being made perfect by the flesh? Have you suffered so many things in vain—if indeed *it was* in vain? Therefore He who supplies the Spirit to you and works miracles among you, *does He do it* by the works of the law, or by the hearing of faith?

There are four kinds of experiences that God uses to shape our lives.

1. He uses personal experiences. The family that you grew up in, The people you relate to. God can use your personal experience with your husband or your wife. He uses personal experiences to shape you.
2. He uses vocational and educational experiences to shape you.
3. He uses spiritual experiences to shape you, like coming to church, or reading your Bible, having a quiet time.
4. He uses painful experiences to shape you.

Ask the person during the conversation: If you take an inventory of your life in starting over, you need to ask yourself three questions.
1. What have I learned?
2. What are my assets? What have I got going for me? Have I got my health? Have I got my freedom? Am I still mentally sound? Have I got some friends? Have I got the Lord? Have I got a church family? What do I have that I can get a fresh start with?
3. Who can help me? When we decide to start fresh in life, we need somebody by our side – a friend, an accountability partner, a support person, or a support group. Find someone that can help you. You need other people because you don't start over by yourself after a major setback or crisis. You need somebody else to walk along with you. There is one that we can count on to be there to help us to start fresh in life. The Lord Jesus will be there, He will help us to pull our lives back together and make sure that we get started on the right foot.

Isaiah 43:19- Behold, I will do a new thing; now it shall spring forth; shall ye not know it? I will even make a way in the wilderness, and rivers in the desert.

1 Corinthians 6:20- For you were bought with a price: therefore glorify God in your body.

I need to take a look at my past. That means I need to evaluate all my Experiences. I need to look At what I have left after the failure.

Galatians 3:3-5- Are you so foolish? Having begun in the Spirit, are you now being made Perfect by the flesh? Have you suffered so many things in vain—if indeed *it was* in vain? Therefore He who supplies the Spirit to you and works miracles among you, *does He do it* by the works of the law, or by the hearing of faith?

Instead of looking to his past, the Apostle Paul concentrated on Christ and what was ahead. Paul listed many of his past sins, but these significant failures did not inhibit his continued growth in Christ. On the other hand, if a believer remembers past sins but is taught to have a blank memory about these failures, a needless tension results that can inhibit one from growing in Christ. A believer can needlessly question, "Why can't I forget my past sins?" and, without knowing it, can place undue attention on past sinfulness at the expense of cooperating with Christ's present work in his or her life.

A believer is burdened with an unnecessary prerequisite for spiritual development if required to "have a blank memory" about past sins. There is no question that past sins can be shameful and painful. However, any past sin does not have to thwart a believer's on-going growth in Christ. The key to being an overcomer is to fix our eyes on Jesus, to rely on God's empowering Holy Spirit, and to follow Scripture with regard to daily living. Instead of having a goal of "being unable to recall" past sins, a believer would find lasting benefit and relief by diligently learning more about the power of the Cross and its effect on daily living. If there was any person whose past sins could have thwarted spiritual progress, it was the Apostle Paul. Yet, he triumphantly proclaimed, "For I decided to know nothing among you except Jesus Christ and him crucified" (**1 Corinthians 2:2**) and "for me to live is Christ and to die is gain" (**Philippians 1:21**). The Apostle Paul's perspective refutes the need to "be unable to recall past sins."

There is no question that sin's consequences often last a lifetime; but there is no act of sin with enough power to overcome the work of Christ and the power of the

Cross in a believer's life. Additionally, trying to achieve a blank memory about one's own sins is not only counterproductive to one's growth in Christ, but it also is unnecessary. Instead, a believer is "to forget" (not take notice) of things behind, both good and bad, in order to press onward toward the goal for the prize of the upward call of God in Christ Jesus. This does not mean that a believer is not to take responsibility for past sins, nor does it mean that restitution for past sins should not be undertaken.

A believer who deals responsibly with the consequences of his or her past sins will NOT be able to "forget" past sins, in the sense of not being able to recall them. Often, the on-going magnitude of sin's consequences will not allow a believer to have a blank memory of past sins (for example, financial support for a child born out of wedlock, or the loss of a marriage due to adultery, or a person injured due to drunk driving). Nevertheless, a believer can still be an overwhelming conqueror in Christ, as Romans chapter 8 clearly proclaims.

In the final analysis, the issue is not a believer's memory of the past that determines effective Christian living and witness. The issue is a believer's commitment to rely on the power of God through His Son, His Word, and His Spirit while concentrating on his or her daily walk in Christ through prayer and meditation, Bible study, obedience to Scripture, fellowship with believers, and ministry to others. The concept of "forgetting your sins" draws attention back to the past, keeping the focus on self rather than Christ. A believer who focuses on the past has taken attention away from the present, the time frame in which spiritual growth takes place. Scripture does not mention this so-called prerequisite for spiritual growth ("forgetting one's sins"). Believers would be wise to redirect their attention to the provisions for spiritual growth as found in God's Word instead of natural, worldly wisdom that lends itself to errors and self-centered perspectives

Learn from your mistakes. Failure can be your friend or your foe. You determine if failure will be your friend or foe by the way you react to it. You can choose to learn from it or choose to repeat it. If you learn from it then it can be your friend. However, if you don't learn from it is your foe.

Jesus makes a very simple statement that relates to a very big problem: our ability to walk away from our old life. This statement to remember Lot's wife is sandwiched between Jesus' discussion on how God's judgment came upon man while he went through his everyday life thinking of the great things he would do tomorrow, but their tomorrow brought only their destruction. And between His discussions on how a changing of our ways will keep us from that destruction.

As we know from Scripture, Lot's wife turned into a pillar of salt after she looked back at the city of Sodom, where she lived, which was being destroyed by the Lord. Now was her punishment because she disobeyed the command given by the angles to not look back as they fled? Or was it because of the reason she looked back? I would say that she was punished for both. God did not want them to look back because He wants us to trust in His direction and future for our lives. When we look back we are saying in our hearts that I miss where I came from and am unsure of where God is leading me.

Genesis 19:26 that Lot's wife looked back and in so doing was turned into a pillar of salt. In this verse we need to understand that the original Hebrew language has the words "looked back" to indicate that she took a longing look upon the city, a look that indicated she wanted what she left and not what God was saving her from or from what new life He was going to give them.

So in looking back to our scripture in Luke we see that Jesus is telling the disciples, as well as us, that we should not be looking back at the things of the world and our old life when He has a better life awaiting us. So don't look back with longing for the life you lived before receiving Christ. **Luke 17:33** "Whosoever shall seek to save his life shall lose it; and whosoever shall lose his life shall preserve it." Again Jesus is letting us know that we need to give up our old ways and look to His ways for our lives. Cast out the old man and let the born-again man live to please our Father in heaven.

When we accepted Christ as our Lord and savior we have signed a contract with Him to follow His lead and not to long for the things of this world, to look forward to the eternal things and not worry so much about the earthly things. In being a disciple of Christ we are to press forward toward the mark that God has set before us. Because when we look back while we are walking we will run into or fall into something. Don't look back; keep an eye on what lays ahead for you.

Let us not distort our old way of life as we lived before the saving grace of Christ lifted us from out of the gutter. Don't look back upon it, but look forward to the wonders that Christ has in store for you. And when you do look back, look back upon what He has done for you to get you where you are today. You may not be where you think you should be, but you are where He wants you to be. Remember that God's ways are not our ways and His thoughts' are not our thoughts'. He has a plan for our lives that we just cannot fully understand. But know that God is unfolding it before your eyes day by day.

For a lot of us we let the guilt of our past life keep us from reaping the rewards of our new life in Christ. Let us not be shackled by the things that we used to do and those things that remain hidden from our past life without Christ. We need to remember that Christ has washed us with His blood and the things that we have done wrong in the past have been forgiven and that we no longer need worry about them surfacing because those things were done in the ignorance of God's grace and those things were done in the ignorance of Jesus' gift of salvation. Remember that those things in our past are washed away and can never be used to shame us, because they were done by the old man. In Christ we are now a new man. And we can see in scriptures that we are not alone in the area of past guilt's':

• Jacob, with the stealing of his brothers birth-right
• Moses, having to deal with his murder of an Egyptian
• Samson, with his continued flaunts with temptation
• David, with the affair and murder • Solomon, with his indulgences with everything worldly
• Peter, with his denial of Jesus

QUESTIONS:

1 **Corinthians 6:20-** For you were _____ with a price: therefore glorify God in your body.

2. Instead of looking to his past, the Apostle Paul concentrated on Christ and What was _____.

3. The concept of "forgetting your sins" draws attention back to the past, Keeping the focus on self rather than Christ. **(T) or (F)**

4. **Philippians 3:12-14**: Not that I have already obtained all this, or have already arrived at my goal, but I press on to take hold of that for which Christ Jesus took hold of me. Brothers and sisters, I do not consider myself yet to have taken hold of it. But one thing I do: _____ what is behind and straining toward what is ahead, I **press** on toward the goal to win the prize for which God has called me heavenward in Christ Jesus

5. **Philippians 3: 12-14**, Apostle Paul made a clear case why as believers, we need to place attention to what is _____us, not what is behind. When you forget your past, you open the door towards a bright new future.

6. Your past is designed to keep you in the _____; but if you press forward, God has Already prepared your future reward. Apostle Paul had a past as Saul the persecutor and prosecutor of brethren but he had to release this old identity, in order for him to move forward in the ministry to which God had called him. Even when he became a believer, he had to get himself to a point when he considered past achievements as dung, in order to completely possess the riches of Christ.

7. Forgiving has to do with forgetting, you can't _____ if you don't forget the Past Forgetting and forgiveness go hand in glove, whether it is forgiving yourself or others. When we forgive, we must _____.

8. When you don't **forgive**, you are living in the _____ and you block the power of God from operating in your life. Not forgiving means you are dwelling firmly in the past. Healing, deliverance, favor and financial breakthrough are _____ when you hold unforgiveness in your heart.

9. As you take inventory of your life, you need to ask yourself (1). What have you learned from past? (2). What is going to change

DOOR TO DOOR TRAINING

TRAINEE SHOULD PARTICIPATE WITH THE INTRODUCTION OF THE OUTLINE

Gospel Introduction

Talk about something in common
Their work
Their neighborhood
Their House
Their Church Background

Transfer into the Gospel by asking them a question

Q1. Ever wish you could wipe away the slate clean and start over?

Q2. Have you thought about that if you died today, would you go to heaven?

Trainees can do their Testimony during this visit.

"S" – STOP MAKING EXCUSES FOR YOUR SIN

"T" - TAKE A LOOK AT YOUR PAST – DID IT HONOR GOD

SESSION #6

"A" ACTIONS SPEAK LOUDER THAN WORDS

PEOPLE WILL DOUBT WHAT YOU SAY UNTIL YOU PROVE IT BY YOUR ACTIONS!

SESSION #6

ACTIONS SPEAK LOUDER THAN WORDS

Colossians 3:17- Whatever you do in word or deed, do all in the name of the Lord Jesus, giving thanks through Him to God the Father.

God's Actions: **John 3:16**- For God so loved the world, that He gave His only begotten son, that whoever believes in Him shall not perish, but have eternal life.

You have to launch out into a new territory. The Bible says that the key to changing anything is **faith**. If you want to change your circumstance, it takes faith.
If you want to change your personality, it takes faith. If you want to change anything in your life, you have to have some faith.

Our Actions Always Speak Louder Than Our Words

Jesus says this in **Matthew 9**. " According to your faith it will be done to you. " That is a very simple statement but it's very powerful. "According to your faith it will be done to you." That means we tend to get out of life what we expect. "According to your faith it will be done to you."

What are you expecting in life? Are things going to be better or worse? Are they going to be the same? If you act in faith then you will do something positive to ensure that you don't repeat the same mistakes over.

The faith that I am talking about is not a dead hope so faith. It is an affirmative faith that takes positive action coupled with the help of God to change your life.

Acts 3:1-5 Now Peter and John went up together into the temple at the hour of prayer, being the ninth hour. And a certain man lame from his mother's womb was carried, whom they laid daily at the gate of the temple which is called Beautiful, to ask alms of them that entered into the temple; Who seeing Peter and John about to go into the temple asked an alms. And Peter, fastening his eyes upon him with John, said, Look on us. And he gave heed unto them, expecting to receive something of them.

This man asked for something and expected to get it, but in reality he got more than he expected. The point that I want to make is this lame man acted in faith and was greatly rewarded. Many times we ask for something and expect to get nothing and we get exactly what we expected, nothing.

In order to start acting in faith that means you've got to stop having a pity party. You've got to stop feeling sorry for yourself. "Poor me! I'm such a victim. Life is unfair." Of course life is unfair! Whoever said it was fair? God never said that. This is a world filled with sin and because of that, life is unfair. But you have to go on with life anyway. You stop having a pity party and stop rehearsing the past, regretting the past, and you get on with the present and the future. The more time we spend regretting our past, the more of our future is wasted. The more time you spend thinking, "I wish that hadn't happened! I wish I could change that. If only I could go back, reverse the clock and redo history," and you're rehearsing and regretting, you'll not only make yourself miserable right now, you're setting yourself up for more of the same thing in the future. The way you set yourself up for more failure is by focusing on past failures. Whatever you focus on you tend to reproduce in your life. "According to your faith it will be done unto you."

What you need to do is learn from those failures. Let me give you the real secret of success. Every successful entrepreneur knows this. **Real success is built on failure.** Failure is the way you become a success. You figure out what doesn't work. When Edison figured out on the 200th or so time, what would make a light bulb stay lit, he did that because he knew 199 ways that didn't work. You never call it a failure in your life. Call it an education. **You learn from past failures and mistakes and act in faith for the future. Some people will never act in faith because they have been paralyzed by the fear of past failures and mistakes.**

PROVERBS 29:25 - The fear of man bringeth a snare: but whoso putteth his trust in the LORD shall be safe

Paul wrote by inspiration to Titus: (**Titus 1:16**) "They profess that they know God; but in works they deny him, being abominable, and disobedient, and unto every good work reprobate." It is sad how many Christians profess to be godly people, but their actions show otherwise. The old saying that actions speak louder than words is surely true!

Not in words but doing good things to brethren **I John 3:17-18** "17. But whoso hath this world's good, and seeth his brother have need, and shutteth up his bowels of compassion from him, how dwelleth the love of God in him?

My little children, let us not love in word, neither in tongue; but in deed and in truth."

We need to be showing by our works- James 3:13 *"Who is a wise man and endued with knowledge among you? let him shew out of a good conversation his works with meekness of wisdom."*

Lip service does not please God Mark 7:6-7 *This people honors Me with their lips, But their heart is far from Me. And in vain they worship Me, Teaching as doctrines the commandments of men*

Hebrews 10:22-26 *"Let us draw near with a true heart in full assurance of faith, having our hearts sprinkled from an evil conscience, and our bodies washed with pure water. Let us hold fast the profession of our faith without wavering; (for he is faithful that promised;) And let us consider one another to provoke unto love and to good works: Not forsaking the assembling of ourselves together, as the manner of some is; but exhorting one another: and so much the more, as ye see the day approaching. For if we sin wilfully after that we have received the knowledge of the truth, there remaineth no more sacrifice for sins."*

The Kingdom should come first Matthew 6:33 *"But seek ye first the kingdom of God, and his righteousness; and all these things shall be added unto you."*

We know the careless by their fruits Matthew 7:15-20 *"Beware of false prophets, which come to you in sheep's clothing, but inwardly they are ravening wolves. Ye shall know them by their fruits. Do men gather grapes of thorns, or figs of thistles? Even so every good tree bringeth forth good fruit; but a corrupt tree bringeth forth evil fruit. A good tree cannot bring forth evil fruit, neither can a corrupt tree bring forth good fruit. Every tree that bringeth not forth good fruit is hewn down, and cast into the fire. Wherefore by their fruits ye shall know them." commandments of men."*

1. You have to launch out into new territory. The Bible says that the key to changing anything is **faith**. If you want to change your circumstance, it takes **faith**.
2. If you want to change your personality, it takes **faith**.
3. If you want to change anything in your life, you have to have some **faith**.
4. **Matthew 9:29** - Then He touched their eyes, saying, "According to your **Faith** let it be to you."
5. What we need to do is learn from the past, act in **faith** for the future and look to God for guidance.

DOOR TO DOOR TRAINING

TRAINEE SHOULD PARTICIPATE WITH THE INTRODUCTION OF THE OUTLINE

Gospel Introduction

Talk about something in common
Their work
Their neighborhood
Their House
Their Church Background

Transfer into the Gospel by asking them a question

Q1.   Ever wish you could wipe away the slate clean and start over?

Q2.   Have you thought about that if you died today, would you go to heaven?

Trainees can do their Testimony during this visit.

"S" – STOP MAKING EXCUSES FOR YOUR SIN

"T" - TAKE A LOOK AT YOUR PAST – DID IT HONOR GOD

"A" - ACTIONS SPEAK LOUDER THAN WORDS

IF LIFE GETS BLURRY – REFOCUS YOUR LIFE

REFOCUS ON THE MAIN THING

SESSION #7

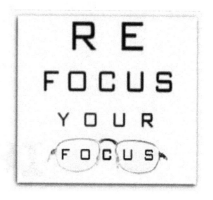

IF LIFE GETS BLURRY – REFOCUS

Matthew 6:33 – But seek ye first the kingdom of God, and his righteousness; and all these things shall be added unto you

I need to refocus my thoughts if I want to change my life. If I want to get going again and start fresh, I need to rethink the way that I think.

Proverbs 4:23- Keep your heart with all diligence, For out of it *spring* the issues of life.

How do you do that? **(1) confession**. You say, "I've confessed to God but I still feel guilty. How do I get rid of a painful memory?" **Not by resisting it but by replacing it. (2) What's the best thing to focus on? God's word**.

The way you think, determines the way you feel. And the way you feel determines the way you act. If you want to change your actions, just change the way you think and it will inevitably change the way you act.

If you are depressed, discouraged and distressed it may be because you're thinking depressed, discouraged and distressing thoughts. That's your choice. You don't have to think those thoughts. If you're acting in fearful, worried ways it's because you're thinking fearful, worried thoughts.

I have to refocus my thoughts to start over, that means I have to stop thinking some old patterns. Which memories are you still rehearsing that keep you from having a fresh start in life? The Bible says **let go**. Let go of those things. The more you hold on to that memory, the more you rehearse it, it continues to hurt you today. It cannot hurt you without your permission. You have to change your mind and let go and get rid of those painful, hurtful memories of shame and guilt and other things.

How do you do that? Confession. You say, "I've confessed to God but I still feel guilty. How do I get rid of a painful memory?" Not by resisting it but by **replacing it**. Not saying, "I'm not going to think about it! I'm not going to think about it!" What are you doing the whole time? Thinking about it. Stop focusing on what you don't want and start focusing on what you do want. Get your attention onto something else. Refocus. Replace those memories by, every time they come up, start thinking about something else.

Psalm 1 - Blessed is the man that **walketh** not in the counsel of the ungodly, nor **standeth** in the way of sinners, nor **sitteth** in the seat of the scornful. But his delight is in the law of the LORD; and in his law doth he **meditate** day and night. And he shall be like a tree planted by the rivers of water, that **bringeth** forth his fruit in his season; his leaf also shall not wither; and whatsoever he doeth shall prosper. The ungodly are not so: but are like the chaff which the wind **driveth** away. Therefore the ungodly shall not stand in the judgment, nor sinners in the congregation of the righteous. For the LORD **knoweth** the way of the righteous: but the way of the ungodly shall perish.

Psalm 1 "Happy OR BLESSED are those who are always meditating on God's word. They're like trees along a river that do not dry up. They succeed in everything they do. "

Those are the two things that everybody wants in life. We all want to be happy and we all want to succeed. The antidote, the answer, the way we get those is the phrase right in the middle " meditating on God's word. " That's the answer to the other two. The more you meditate on God's word, the happier and more successful you'll be in Your Christian life. It's a promise from God. Meditating on God's word simply means rehearsing God's word in our minds.

It's interesting that the Bible does not say, "If you read this book, you'll be happy and successful." It does not say, "If you listen to this book, like through a sermon, you'll be happy and successful." It says, "If you meditate on it you'll be happy and successful." In meditating it means I think on it over and over and what it means in my life. I consider it and consider its implications for my life. As we fill our mind with God's word, it begins to change our mind. We stop seeing ourselves as other people see us or as we have seen ourselves and we begin to see ourselves as God does. That's where the change takes place. That's the power to start over.

QUESTIONS:

1. What do you do when you feel that your life is out of focus?
    _____

2. I need to refocus my thoughts if I want to change my life. (T) or (F)

3. If I want to get going again and start fresh, I need to rethink the way that I think. (T) or (F)

4. **Proverbs 4:23**- Keep your **heart** with all diligence, For out of it *spring* the issues of life.

5. How do you refocus your life? _____

6. The way you think, determines the way you **feel.** And the way you feel determines the way you **act**. If you want to change your actions, just change the way you think and it will inevitably change the way you **act**.

7. **Psalm 1** -   [1]Blessed is the man that walketh not in the counsel of the ungodly, Nor standeth in the way of sinners, nor sitteth in the seat of the scornful. But his delight is in the law of the LORD; and in his law doth he meditate day and night.

8. What does it mean to live daily as a Christian and be committed to the small things? _____

9. What are the important things that people aim for in life? Own home/ Financial freedom/ healthy/ happy. _____

10. But how important are they to God? _____

11. Are we Keeping the Main Thing the Main thing?_____

11. Since Jesus very clearly taught that the most important thing to do in obedience to God is to keep HIM first above ALL other THINGS; to love Him with ALL of our hearts, souls, minds, and strength, and to love others as we love ourselves; Jesus is supposed to be the main thing in our lives. But is He? _____!

12. How do we recognize the importance of Jesus' instructions when we read Matthew 6:21, which says "For where your treasure is, there your heart will be Also" _____

DOOR TO DOOR TRAINING

TRAINEE SHOULD PARTICIPATE WITH THE INTRODUCTION OF THE OUTLINE

Gospel Introduction

Talk about something in common
Their work
Their neighborhood
Their House
Their Church Background

Transfer into the Gospel by asking them a question

Q1.   Ever wish you could wipe away the slate clean and start over?

Q2.   Have you thought about that if you died today, would you go to heaven?

Trainees can do their Testimony during this visit.

"S" – STOP MAKING EXCUSES FOR YOUR SIN

"T" - TAKE A LOOK AT YOUR PAST – DID IT HONOR GOD

"A" - ACTIONS SPEAK LOUDER THAN WORDS

"R" - IF LIFE GETS BLURRY- REFOCUS

DRAWING THE NET

WHO ARE YOU GOING TO TRUST?

SESSION #8

T- WHO ARE YOU GOING TO TRUST

WHO ARE YOU GOING TO **T**RUST? GOD? OR THIS WORLD?

Doing the same thing over and over and over and expecting different results. If we keep doing the same thing then we will keep getting the same result.

We can't change who we are, only God can do that. I am not speaking about the outward man but the inner man. The real person is the hidden person of the heart. Success in life is not trying harder, but living smarter. Giving God control of my life.

If we will... * **A-** accept the sacrifice that was made for us

* **C-** confess our sins to God

* **T-** turn away (repent) of those sins and

then... * **go forward, obeying His Word.** We are promised an eternal home in Heaven with Him

Isaiah 43:20- The beast of the field shall honour me, the dragons and the owls: because I give waters in the wilderness, and rivers in the desert, to give drink to my people, my chosen.

Zechariah 4:6 - Then he answered and spake unto me, saying, This is the word of the LORD unto Zerubbabel, saying, Not by might, nor by power, but by my spirit, saith the LORD of hosts.

"When someone becomes a Christian, They become a brand new person inside. He is not the same anymore. A new life has begun!" God specializes in new beginnings.

Jesus Christ has the power to do that. It's called being born again, the chance to start over. We can start fresh with a new life as we begin this New Year. God says, "I don't want you to turn over a new leaf. I'm going to give you a whole new life."

Trust God to help us succeed. Depend on Him. We don't need to depend on ourselves. We've already proven that we can't do it on our own. That's why we've failed. Some people just don't get it. They stumble and fall and then they get up and say, "I'll just try harder!" It's like you go up to a wall and bang your head against it and the wall doesn't fall down. You try it again and Bang! Again. You keep doing it thinking, "Maybe it will fall over this time." That's the definition of insanity – doing the same thing over and over and over and expecting different results.

If we keep doing the same thing then we will keep getting the same result. We can't change who we are, only God can do that.

I am not speaking about the outward man but the inner man. The real person is the hidden person of the heart. Success in the Christian life is not trying harder but living smarter. Giving God control of my life.

One of the greatest challenges of trust is that trusting God means we believe what we cannot see. It means God is at work carrying out His purposes even when we do not see evidence of Him working in our lives. **Hebrews 11:1** tells us "Faith is being sure of what we hope for and certain of what we do not see." And trust is the basis of faith.

Consider Noah who "built a ship in the middle of dry land". **Hebrews 11:7**- "He was warned about something he couldn't see, and acted on what he was told".

And then there was Abraham. Verses 8 through 10 tell us that because Abraham trusted God, he had faith to say "yes to God's call to travel to an unknown place that would become his home. When he left he had no idea where he was going. By an act of faith he lived in the country promised him, lived as a stranger camping in tents. . . . Abraham did it by keeping his eye on an unseen city with real, eternal foundations—the City designed and built by God".

Moses, too, trusted in the invisible. I'm sure when he came to the Red Sea, he had no idea how they were going to cross until he raised his staff over the water as God had instructed.

Hebrews 11:6: "Without faith it is impossible to please God: for he that cometh to God must believe that He is (that God exists), and that He is a rewarder of them that diligently seek Him."

God IS a rewarder of them that diligently seek Him. Not those who seek merely His blessings, but those who seek Him, are the ones who find their reward. For He is the reward.

All action is dependent on belief. In other words, if you believe something, you will act on it. If you don't believe it, you will not act on it.

God is bringing us to a decision: Do we trust God or do we trust in "man"?

Questions:

1. Who should we acknowledge Jesus to? (**_Other people_**)

2. When we acknowledge Jesus before men, to whom will Jesus acknowledge us? _____

3. Why do you believe Jesus says that we must acknowledge or confess Him before others? _____

4. What may happen if we don't acknowledge or confess Jesus? (**_He will not acknowledge us before God._**)

5. Is it enough to simply state that Jesus is who he says he is? _____
_____

6. **Read Acts 2:37-47 -** Why does Peter say "repent" in verse 38? What Does "repent" mean? **To turn from -** _____
_____

7. What else does Peter suggest the people do besides repenting of their sin? **_To be_** _____

8. What is promised to the people if they do what Peter suggests?

_____

9. Peter lets the crowd know who can be saved. Who? _____
_____

10. Do you believe the Lord is calling you? _____.

11. What changes took place in the lives of the new believers? (look through verses 42-47 what do you see?)

A. They gave _____ to God
B. They had _____ with each other
C. They were _____ with awe
D. They _____ together
E. They _____themselves to the apostles teaching
F. They saw many _____ and miraculous signs done by the Apostles
G. They had everything in _____
H. They _____to anyone who had a need

DOOR TO DOOR TRAINING

TRAINEE SHOULD PARTICIPATE WITH THE INTRODUCTION OF THE OUTLINE

Gospel Introduction

Talk about something in common
        Their work
        Their neighborhood
        Their House
        Their Church Background

Transfer into the Gospel by asking them a question

Q1.   Ever wish you could wipe away the slate clean and start over?

Q2.   Have you thought about that if you died today, would you go to heaven?

Trainees can do their Testimony during this visit.

"S" – STOP MAKING EXCUSES FOR YOUR SIN

"T" - TAKE A LOOK AT YOUR PAST – DID IT HONOR GOD

"A" - ACTIONS SPEAK LOUDER THAN WORDS

"R" - IF LIFE GETS BLURRY- REFOCUS

"T" - WHO ARE YOU GOING TO TRUST???

SINNERS PRAYER

ALSO THE FOLLOW UP.

SESSION #9

OUR RESPONSE TO JESUS

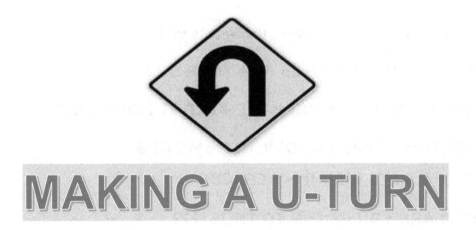

MAKING A U-TURN

SESSION #9

Our Response is to receive Jesus

We must repent of our sin.
Acts 3:19- Repent, then, and turn to God, so that your sins may be wiped out

   Repentance is not just feeling sorry for our sin. Repentance is turning to God through Jesus and turning away from our sin. It is like making a U-Turn.

   We must place our faith in Jesus. Ephesians 2:8- For it is by grace you have been saved through faith- and this not from yourselves, it is the gift of God.

 **Faith is trusting in Jesus Christ alone for eternal life!**

HERE ARE SOME IMPORTANT QUESTIONS TO THINK ABOUT:

1. **Does this make sense to you?**

2. **Are you ready to start fresh in your life?**

3. **Are you willing to place your faith in Jesus right now and turn from your sin?**

Romans 10:13 – For Everyone who calls on the name of the Lord will be saved.

If that is your decision right now – Then ask the Lord to save you.

Then this is what you need to do:

The Bible says in **Romans 10:13**, "For whosoever shall call upon the name of the Lord shall be saved."

"Whosoever" means you. We could put your name there: "For (your name) shall call upon the name of the Lord and (your name) shall be saved."

Now, if you will trust the Lord Jesus Christ to save you from your sins and take you to Heaven when you die, just bow your head and close your eyes. If you mean this with all your heart, pray this prayer believing:

PRAYER:

"Dear Lord Jesus, please have mercy on me, and forgive my sins. I put my trust in you Lord Jesus to cleanse me from all of my sins by your blood. Please give me the free gift of eternal life. Thank you for your promise to take me to heaven when I die and for saving me, Amen."

Congratulations!

If you just prayed that prayer and meant it in your heart, you can know you are going to Heaven for the Bible promises in **John 3:36,** "He that believeth on the Son (Jesus) hath everlasting life." And in **Acts 16:31,** "Believe on the Lord Jesus Christ and thou shalt be saved...."

WELCOME TO THE FAMILY OF GOD

If you sincerely prayed this prayer, you have just made the most important decision of your life. You can be sure you are saved and have eternal life.

AS YOU START FRESH TODAY

Jesus wants to do more than just reside in your heart. He wants to be Lord of your life.

Romans 10:9-10- that if you confess with your mouth the Lord Jesus and believe in your heart that God has raised Him from the dead, you will be saved. For with the heart one believes unto righteousness, and with the mouth confession is made unto salvation.

ASSURANCE

You know you have Eternal Life because God loves you and He keeps His promises:

- You repented of your sins **Acts 3:19**- Repent ye therefore, and be converted, that your sins maybe blotted out, when the times of refreshing shall come from the presence of the Lord.
- You placed your faith in Jesus **Ephesians 2:8-9**- For by Grace are ye saved through faith; and that not of yourselves: it is the Gift of God: Not of works, lest any man should boast.

God heard your prayer and recorded it

Romans 10:13- For whosoever shall call upon the name of the Lord shall be saved.

How do we grow spiritually

- Speak with God through prayer
- Study God's Word – The Bible
- Be with God's people in worship and fellowship
- Tell others about Christ

The Bible

Read one chapter in the bible each day. Begin with the book of John.

Psalm 119:105- Your word *is* a lamp to my feet And a light to my path
1 Peter 2:2 - as newborn babes, desire the pure milk of the word, that you may grow thereby

WORSHIP

Worship regularly in a church that teaches you the Bible. Worship is vital to spiritual growth. **John 4:23**- But the hour is coming, and now is, when the true worshipers will worship the Father in spirit and truth; for the Father is seeking such to worship Him

Psalm 34:1- I will bless the LORD at all times; His praise *shall* continually *be* in my mouth.

2 Important means of worship are Baptism and the Lord's Supper

Baptism – Is the sign that believers give to the world regarding our personal relationship to God through Jesus Christ. All Christians are commanded to be baptized.

The Lord's Supper- Is a time of reflections upon the great sacrifice of the Lord Jesus Made for us. The broken bread reminds us of His physical body that was wounded for us. The cup we drink is a reminder of His blood He shed for us.

THIS IS A NEW DAY TO START FRESH

1 John 4:4- The one who is in you is greater than the one who is in the world.

There is one that didn't like your decision today. Jesus says there is an enemy – The thief comes only to steal and kill and destroy – **John 10:10**

Satan could not stop you from your decision today in receiving Christ as your Lord and Savior. So he will try to keep you from becoming joyful and a happy effective follower of Christ.

You know what? You have a friend and a protector. **Proverbs 18:24**- A man *who has* friends must himself be friendly, But there is a friend *who* sticks closer than a brother

Matthew 28:20- teaching them to observe all things that I have commanded you; and lo, I am with you always, *even* to the end of the age." Amen.

So with God anything is possible. Go out and Start Fresh with your life with Christ.

AFTER THE TEAM LEAVES THE HOUSE

After You Have Left the Home Take good notes about the homes you've visited. Don't rely on your memory! As soon as you get the chance, record what happened at the home. However, do not write notes about the people while standing in their driveway right after you have talked with them. Wait till you have left the premises, are out of eyesight, or until you are in your car.

Write the notes on the Map page or Visit info page on your way back to the church. There should be someone there to retrieve them from your team. Remember **Titus 3:14** says, "And let ours also learn to maintain good works for necessary uses, that they be not unfruitful."

Live with an eternal purpose in mind. Win souls. Gather people to take with you in the soon coming harvest

Thank you for being a part of Start Fresh Ministry. I hope you see that through the entire bible, we are all supposed to share the Gospel. With the Start Fresh outline, you will be able to feel secure in what to say. From sharing with a waitress at a restaurant, to a coworker at work, to a family member.

Make this outline your own. Make this outline to be used every day to everyone you see. Let's all do our part and let the Holy Spirit lead you to be bold in sharing the Gospel.

Thank you for a passion for lost people and I challenge you to give your time, your heart and a love for Jesus.

Thank you!

Bo Ambrose

START FRESH VISITATION FORM

NAME:_____   VISITING TEAM_____

ADDRESS: _____   DATE: _____

CITY/STATE/ ZIP:_____

<u>AGE GROUPS</u>
<u>18 & UNDER</u> ___   19-25: ___   26-40: ___   41-55:___   56-64: ___   65+___

<u>CHILDREN:</u>
NAME:_____   AGE:____
NAME:_____   AGE:_____
NAME:_____   AGE:_____
NAME:_____   AGE:_____

CHURCH THAT THEY ATTEND?_____

<u>PLEASE CHECK ALL THAT APPLY:</u>
FIRST TIME VISITOR _____
RETURNING VISITOR_____
WOULD LIKE TO KNOW MORE ABOUT THE CHURCH _____
NEW RESIDENT_____

<u>OUTLINE</u>   WHAT DID YOU SHARE TONIGHT?
INTRODUCTION
Q1 AND Q2
STOP MAKING EXCUSES
TAKE A LOOK AT YOUR PAST
ACTIONS SPEAK LOUDER THAN WORDS
REFOCUS
TRUST

DID THEY CCEPT CHRIST_____   FOLLOW UP DATE_____
INVITE TO CHURCH _____

ABOUT THE AUTHOR

Bo Ambrose is the founder of Start Fresh Evangelism. Start Fresh Evangelism is a ministry that started in 2015 for the main purpose of training people to share the gospel in their community. He is a Jail Minister, a Sunday School teacher and has a passion to share Christ.

One Tuesday evening at the Knoxville Detention Facility having a church service with the inmates, teaching on "Starting Fresh", 8 men came to know Christ. God was in the jail house that night.

As he was walking down the hallway of the jail, a conversation with God began. God said to write it. "Write what"? By the time he got to the outside, there was a clear picture of what to write. This book was it.

Bo Ambrose
Start Fresh Evangelism
hoistcraneman@aol.com

CPSIA information can be obtained
at www.ICGtesting.com
Printed in the USA
LVHW01s2323220318
570898LV00002B/2/P

9 781945 698507